MW01716907

THE PROPAGANDA SHIELD

YOU RECOGNIZE THE INDOCTRINATION. NOW DISARM IT.

WILSON STOOKSBERRY

Book Design by HMDPublishing.com

DEDICATION

To my grandfathers, Rollin Wilson and Walter Stooksberry. They were both God-fearing patriots, World War II veterans, and decades ahead of their time when it came to spotting surround-sound nonsense. They gave me my first lessons in seeing through the noise. I owe them more than I can say.

ACKNOWLEDGMENTS

Endless thanks to my wife, Gillian... for enduring the strange hours, relentless keyboard noise, and the occasional manic energy of a man trying to untangle the world's madness. You're a saint for putting up with it.

PREFACE

I never set out to write a book. I wrote a simple outline on social media. It described how propaganda functions and how citizens might arm themselves against it. It was direct, unapologetic, and grounded in reality. To my surprise, it resonated. It spread quickly.

Not long after I had written it, a call came in from an NFL Pro Bowler. He was calling as a father, disturbed by what his children were being taught, what they were absorbing from their schools and screens etc. He didn't ask for slogans or bromides. He asked for a curriculum—something enduring and real that could anchor young minds in truth and equip them to resist the barrage of lies dressed up as compassion and progress.

I originally generated an online class with his children in mind. But very quickly, the work outgrew that narrow purpose. Because this wasn't merely a crisis of childhood education—it was a crisis of citizenship. The tools I was building proved just as vital for parents, teachers, teenagers, and everyday Americans battered by the same psychological operations.

This is not an academic work. I didn't write it for tenure committees or to genuflect before gatekeepers. I wrote it for my neighbors, friends, and family—those who grit their teeth as familiar faces fall prey to smooth-talking manipulators, who instinctively recoil at the hollow jargon of modern ideology.

If you've ever watched a lie masquerade as virtue, cowardice sold as compassion, or obedience as intelligence—then this book is for you.

You don't need advanced degrees or government sanction to guard your mind. You need clarity. You need courage. You need tools.

This book provides them.

The rest depends on you.

– Wilson Stooksberry

GRAB YOUR FREE GIFT!

Get ahead of the game by downloading the companion workbook for this edition of the book.

This bonus will help you put these principles into practice and make the content even more valuable for your daily life. Here's how to get it:

1. Go Here: propagandashield.com/free-gift

OR use QR CODE:

(Retails for $29.95 ... Yours FREE!)

2. Tell us where to email the access link
3. Check your email, then use link to access the document
4. Have fun following along as you read the book

(Offer available to readers only. I may change or update the bonus over time, but it will always be something designed to support and strengthen what you've learned in these pages.)

Contents

SECTION III - THE NUMBERS CAN LIE

SECTION IV - NAVIGATING THE MODERN PROPAGANDA LANDSCAPE

INTRODUCTION: YOU'RE THE FIREWALL AGAINST THE MADNESS

A once-cheerful neighbor turned savage, hacking his neighbors to death with a machete. He'd borrowed a stick of butter from them only a week earlier. What happened? An influencer told him they were the enemy.

Teachers, influencers, and algorithms tell a 12-year-old boy that his instincts are dangerous. Because he's male, they brand him part of the problem. He learns to stay quiet, head down, ashamed for simply existing.

A modern mom feels like she's failing, torn between what she knows her kids need and what the credentialed 'parenting experts' demand. Ideological advice floods her feed, not truth. They mock her instincts and wreck her confidence.

None of these are hypotheticals. They're real-world examples of coordinated messages doing their job. Not just influencing people but reshaping their reality.

More real-world examples:

Children reported their parents to the government because they lacked loyalty to the regime. The government either imprisons or executes the parents. The children are then praised for their bravery.

A 16-year-old girl learns that empowerment means putting everything on display. She's told that attention equals love. The more provocative, the more powerful. Her innocence pays the price.

A 28-year-old shrugs at the idea of marriage or children. "The planet's doomed anyway," he says. He's not broken. He's been convinced that life itself is selfish.

You get the point.

There are plenty of books about propaganda—some are academic, some historical, some ideological.

This isn't any of those. This one is different.

This book has a single purpose:

To protect your heart and mind from destructive messaging—and those of the people you love.

It's about building confidence, sharpening your defenses, and learning how to spot and resist deceit. In a genuinely free country, you can't silence the propagandists.

But you can poison their well.

That's what this book is here to help you do.

It's a shield. And it was built for this exact moment in time.

Why now? Because the messages have never been as loud, relentless, and omnipresent as they are right now.

They come from government podiums, TikTok trends, brand slogans, and school curricula. They crawl through the cracks in your phone screen. They don't argue. They frame. They flatter. They distort. They omit. And they do it so well that we don't even realize we're being programmed.

To wit, that's what happened in Rwanda.

That genocidal insanity didn't begin with machetes. It started with humorous messaging from an influencer. That was in 1994, when their 'influencer' was just a DJ on the radio.

I Wasn't Looking for This Fight

What brought me to this strange battlefield? Long story short: I was just a guy trying to make sense of the madness after 9/11.

That day altered countless lives (mine included). Everyone remembers the towers falling, but what stayed with me most was the loss of something deeper: our sense of stability. The illusion that we were safe and understood the world disappeared overnight. In the aftermath, the media wasted no time shaping the national mood. I expected propaganda from our nation's enemies, but what caught my attention was our domestic news coverage in the USA. The messaging at home felt calculated. The so-called battle between George W. Bush and the "liberal press" dominated headlines, but it all seemed like noise; left vs. right, hawk vs. dove, while something deeper was happening underneath.

I couldn't name it yet. But I could feel it.

This wasn't all abstract to me. My grandfather served on the U.S. Army staff during the Nuremberg trials at the end of World War II. He told me stories about working adjacent to the psychological teams tasked with turning former Hitler Youth back into Pfadfinder (the German equivalent of Boy Scouts). His stories gave me an early, unfiltered look at how deep psychological warfare runs, and how powerful it can be when used to build or to destroy nations.

Eventually, I joined the new 21st-century fight. The 'War on Terror' needed bodies, and I volunteered. I earned a place in U.S. Air Force Pararescue, one of the US military's most punishing special operations training pipelines.

But before I stepped into the "Indoctrination course" (yes, actual course name), I did something a bit eccentric for my preparation: I hit the psychology books.

I didn't want the military to indoctrinate me without my awareness and approval.

I wanted to understand the mechanism of mind-shaping.

That season of self-education kicked my understanding of psychological indoctrination into overdrive.

I made it through the training, one of only five who remained out of the original 120. It was brutal. Our cadre pushed us through psych-breaking drills, forcing us to swim underwater for long stretches fully clothed and endure survival exercises like 'drownproofing.'

The program used those exercises and sleepless nights to trigger panic and expose weakness. But I wasn't just a participant in all that ... I was an intense observer of it. I watched how the system broke us down and rebuilt us, step by step, with calculated precision. It wasn't chaos. It was an engineered transformation.

What started as training preparation became a two-decade obsession. I devoured everything: Nuremberg, Madison Avenue, military psyops, counterinsurgency strategy, especially the "hearts and minds" doctrine within it.

This book isn't theory. It's hard-earned knowledge. It's how I forged my shield, one trial at a time.

I'm now handing it to you.

What This Book Is (And Isn't)

Before we dive into what's ahead, I should make something clear:

This isn't a book that claims to show you *the Truth.*

This book helps you *detect deceit* (whether it shows up in ads, news, political spin, or conversation).

If you're serious about finding Truth, learn to spot deception (especially the lies you tell yourself!). We're all guilty of it. By the end of this book, you'll have the tools to cut through the lies, both around you and within you.

This isn't a partisan hit job, either. It's not here to prop up one political party or tear another down. You will find plenty of hogwash in every social order built by humans.

What will happen is simple:

The more propaganda a person or movement uses, the more naked they'll look by the time you finish reading.

Some movements and people will be exposed harder than others, but that depends on them (not this book).

I'm not here to play favorites. Most examples intentionally avoid modern politics or religious sects to bypass the presuppositional baggage we all carry.

I'll give more than one example when current events show up, so every political tribe has a reason to be annoyed. No one gets a pass.

What matters is this: you'll walk away with the core principles behind how deception works in messaging. That's the mission.

I'm here to hand you the flashlight. What you point it at is up to you.

The Game Plan

This book will walk you through 4 sections to complete the construction of your shield:

1. **Foundations of Propaganda:** Where it came from, how it works, why it's everywhere.
2. **Classic Techniques:** Rhetorical sleight-of-hand, logical fallacies, and more.
3. **Statistical Deception:** How Numbers Are Weaponized.
4. **Modern Propaganda:** Internet, AI, social media, and who pulls their strings?

Your understanding of each section is vital. Each section builds on the last. By the end, you'll be able to see through the tricks, teach your loved ones to do the same, and stand your ground.

I've written this book to be punchy and no-fluff. Social media has trained all of us to have zero patience for filler, so I've cut it. The format will feel more like a technical manual than a typical book in many places. That's on purpose. My goal is simple: deliver the most value in the fewest words possible.

The First Trick

Propaganda rarely shouts. It usually hides, dressed as something helpful, harmless, or even noble.

We don't notice it. We applaud it. And then we obey.

Edward Bernays, the father of modern public relations, understood this better than anyone.[1]

Philip Morris asked Bernays to help double their market. The problem? Society treated women smoking as taboo, thus most women didn't smoke...

So, what did he do?

---

1 David Hoffman, *He said cigarettes to women are "Torches of Freedom"*, YouTube video, posted Nov 16, 2014, https://www.youtube.com/watch?v=SRjbXiwN-VDc&t=2s

He went to a psychoanalyst, Dr. A.A. Brill, and asked what cigarettes symbolized to women. The answer? "Torches of freedom."[2]

Bernays then organized a publicity stunt during the Easter Parade in New York. He hired debutantes to light up cigarettes in public. The press was tipped off, and the cameras rolled.

In one move, he reframed smoking from a male vice to a feminist empowerment statement.

Within six weeks, the taboo was fully shattered. The market doubled. Millions would die of cancer because of a psychological magic trick.

That's the power of propaganda.

You'll start spotting this framing trick everywhere. It gets copy-pasted into nearly every major public issue. Recognizing it now will save you a staggering amount of time, money, and grief. You will be fully prepared to recognize this framing and many other mental cons by the end of this book.

Why You're Critical to the Mission

You're not here to manipulate. You're here to protect yourself and your loved ones.

If you've made it this far, you don't need any more convincing that the world has drifted into something hollow, synthetic, and insane. You're not imagining it. Slogans have replaced thought. Mindless distractions have replaced peace. The 'zombie problem' ...that problem that you feel in your bones (but can't exactly explain) ...that's *real.*

But it's not irreversible.

If enough people recognized the hidden battlefield AND understood the defense tactics laid out in this book, and practiced them, we could 'stop the spread' (lol, we'll explain sloganeering later). Parents, teachers, mentors, and everyday citizens could use this material to change the trajectory of entire communities. You can put this knowledge into your own words and share it in your own way, or hand this book to someone. If every reader taught just one other person how to see through the fog, their ripple effect could change the world.

2 David Hoffman, *He Said Cigarettes to Women Are "Torches of Freedom"*, YouTube video, 2:59, posted November 16, 2014, https://www.youtube.com/watch?v=PaD2E5JxF_U.

That's not an exaggeration, it's just math.

You're not just reading a book. You're owning a problem that affects all of us, even the ones who think you're crazy for questioning norms. In a world this upside down, clear-headed people are rare. But they're vital. Survival depends on them. On you. So, thank you for being one of the few.

Now ... let's build your shield and change the world.

SECTION I - LAYING THE GROUNDWORK

CHAPTER 1:
The Con Job: How Propaganda Hacks Your Brain

Picture Captain America raising his shield, deflecting incoming fire. That's the image I want in your head. We're about to build something like it.

But these bullets aren't made of lead.

They're made of headlines, hashtags, slogans, and half-truths in AI answers.

They don't aim for your body.

They aim for your beliefs.

Some come dressed as news. Some as helpful advice. Some, like the one that almost got me today, wear the face of an old friend.

Let's break it down.

A Shield Needs to Be Tougher Than the Attack

Today, I saw a Facebook post from an old buddy. You may have seen a post like it, but it was a brand-new strategy at the time I saw it. It said his dad was going into a care home and they were selling personal items—everything from furniture to a pristine F-150 for a deep discount. I got emotional. I liked that man's dad. Then I saw the truck. Fire sale price. My emotions started running the show: concern for the family, fear of missing out. I DM'd my friend.

Then came the request for a "refundable deposit" from my "friend" through his response. That's when it immediately hit me.

I froze. Blinking. Then I labeled it: *FOMO ('fear of missing out').* That single act, naming the emotion, snapped me out of it.

This is the first part of your shield: **naming the emotion**. It's called *affect labeling*, and it's backed by real science. Label the feeling, and you now have a fighting chance to regain control.

Propaganda Is a Con

A con artist doesn't merely lie—the best ones manipulate you emotionally, so you skip the rational thinking part of making a decision. Propaganda does the same thing on a mass scale. The Institute for Propaganda Analysis (IPA), the OG 'Propaganda Shield' course of the 1930s, knew this 100 years ago. They warned us that if you can shortcut the logical part of the brain and trigger the emotional part, you can control people.

They were right, but some scholars have argued that the IPA wasn't effective in their campaign to teach citizens to protect themselves from propaganda.'[3]

The IPA outlined basic techniques—such as name-calling and glittering generalities—but left the deeper layers of emotional manipulation untouched. At best, they handed you labels for the tools being used on you, without offering any real defense against them. Fast-forward to now: even NATO blatantly admits the geopolitical battlefield is primarily concerned with information warfare as much as anything else.

In a 2023 report, they echoed what has been the 'scientific consensus' about our behavioral norms as human beings: only 5 to 10% of human decisions are rational. The rest? Emotion. Repetition. Bias. Fallacy.[4]

Translation?
You don't need tanks if you can hijack the mind.
And democracy doesn't mean much if mass media can steer the herd with feelings instead of facts.

---

3 Tim Wood, "Propaganda, Obviously: How Propaganda Analysis Fixates on the Hidden and Misses the Conspicuous," Harvard Kennedy School Misinformation Review 2, no. 2 (April 2021),

4 Commander Cornelis van der Klaauw, "Cognitive Warfare," The Three Swords Magazine, no. 39 (2023): 97.

The SOLUTION: An algorithm called NESTPAD

The military loves acronyms, for good reason. In high-stress situations, they help simplify complex actions into something you can remember. Take battlefield trauma, for instance. When someone's injured under fire, you can't afford to freeze. You need a clear sequence. That's where S-MARCH comes in: **Shoot back or stop the threat**, check for **Massive hemorrhage**, ensure a clear **Airway**, evaluate **Respiratory function**, monitor **Circulation**, and assess for **Head injuries and Heat loss**.

In the same way, fighting propaganda demands a mental battle plan. That's why we created **NESTPAD**—our cognitive combat acronym. Here's its breakdown:

- **N**ame the **E**motion (Affect Labeling)
- **S**ay the **T**echnique (e.g., "This is a strawman")
- **P**rove the Claim
- **A**nd
- **D**isprove the claim

You'll hear NESTPAD a thousand times throughout this book because it works.

In today's con, I caught myself at step one. That's all it took to stop the manipulation cold. But the deeper you go with NESTPAD, the stronger your shield becomes.

Why Naming Works

As shown in the NESTPAD algorithm, the first 2 steps involve naming:

1. The **emotion** the message triggered
2. The **technique** being used

When you name a feeling, like FOMO, fear, or shame, you disrupt the autopilot that propaganda depends on. The same goes for technique labeling. The moment you say, "That's an assertion stated as a fact," you've already weakened its power by calling it out. The bulk of this book is about **learning** those techniques. You can't do the 'ST' in our system if you don't know what to look for. But don't worry—learning them is fun. Recognizing these techniques can help rewire your brain. Sounds wild, right? Try it. Many people who've taken this course say it changed how they see everything.

Naming reduces the con's power. Period.

Where We're Going Next

After learning the most common techniques, we'll keep building the shield by learning to dissect modern media and rehearse NESTPAD until it becomes second nature. You're not just protecting yourself—you're becoming a guardian of your entire household's mental sovereignty.

The next chapter lays out why this material doesn't belong in niche corners of the internet; it needs to go mainstream, fast.

Keep moving forward!

CHAPTER 2:

The Wreckage: Why Propaganda Is as Dangerous As War

There's one truth almost all human beings can agree on: war is terrible. Whether you've been to war or only seen it in documentaries, you know the devastation. The leveled cities, broken bodies, and lost lives are the stuff of nightmares.

Would you believe me if I said propaganda can wreck lives just as effectively as bombs?
Not with shrapnel, but with lies, distortion, and psychological warfare.
This chapter exists to make you *feel* that reality, not just understand it.

We launched this book with examples of how destructive propaganda can be. Let's drive the point home.

The Parable of Propaganda Boy

Stories stick better than lectures. This one's about two brothers: Nice Nick and Devil Dave.

One morning, Devil Dave snaps and beats Nick senseless. But just before Nick can defend himself, Dave pulls out his phone and starts recording. He captures only the part where Nick strikes back. Then he streams it live.

Snapchat friends see a violent Nick. Dave rushes to their parents, crying and bleeding. First to report wins. When Nick gets to school, the damage is done—he's the villain. The story is set.

Nick loses friends. Gets grounded. Loses confidence. The good path he was on derails. He spirals. Meanwhile, friends and family reward Devil Dave with sympathy, social points, and a free pass to do it again.

This story is fiction. But the tactic? Very real.

What Just Happened?

This is textbook propaganda. The' half-truth' technique (aka the 'contextomy') is a perception hack. It's one of the many techniques that you will be able to spot naturally after reading this book. It's the same psychological sleight of hand used in global media, politics, and marketing every day.

The damage? Devastating. In the story, a false narrative permanently derails Nick's life. Now scale that up.

Propaganda Without Resources: Still Deadly

Devil Dave had nothing but a smartphone and lies. Still, he rewrote reality. That's the takeaway: even low-tech propaganda can destroy lives.

Now ask yourself—what happens when propaganda *has* resources?

Propaganda With Power: Vietnam and the Holodomor

Vietnam War – Sparked by what we now know was likely a false flag: the Gulf of Tonkin incident. U.S. leadership told us that the North Vietnamese attacked our ship. Declassified documents and historical accounts now strongly suggest otherwise.[5] That lie may have cost 60,000 American lives and hundreds of thousands more worldwide.

The Holodomor – One of the largest man-made famines in history. Millions starved to death in Ukraine in the 1930s. But it didn't start with bullets. It began with propaganda, portraying Ukrainian farmers (kulaks) as greedy traitors. The Soviet machine justified atrocity by narrative. note: Holdovers still justify the starvation by simply calling it a 'drought' that has been politicized.

---

5 Pat Paterson, "The Truth About Tonkin," Naval History 22, no. 1 (February 2008), U.S. Naval Institute. https://www.usni.org/magazines/naval-history-magazine/2008/february/truth-about-tonkin.

You don't murder millions without selling the story first.

Democide: Death by Government, Sold Through Lies

The biggest killer of the 20th century wasn't war. It was government-led murder—*democide*. Communism led the way. But again, death wasn't the first step. Propaganda was.

This should shake you.

Why This Lesson Matters

Propaganda isn't just annoying. It's not just inconvenient. It's not just "bad messaging." It's a force that destroys futures, *starts* wars, mangles bodies, derails truth, and rewrites history.

I want you to feel the weight of what lies can unleash—the ripple effect of distortion, the wreckage it leaves behind.
Because once you *feel* what propaganda can do, you'll start to fight it for yourself, your loved ones, and your neighbors.

Let's keep forging the shield.
You're going to need it, and so is your country.

CHAPTER 3:
Breaking Down the Bullet: What Propaganda Is and How It Hits You

You remember the NATO think tank quote from earlier, right? The one that said (on average) 90–95% of our decisions aren't rational? That they come from bias, habit, and emotion? Let's dig deeper into why that matters—and how propaganda uses it to hijack you.

Defining the Weapon

Let's get clear on terms. If propaganda is going to be the bullet we're shielding against, we need to understand how it works.

Edward Bernays, the "Father of Public Relations," defined propaganda as:

> *"The conscious and intelligent manipulation of the organized habits and opinions of the masses."*

He didn't stop there. He added:

> *"Those who manipulate this unseen mechanism of society constitute an invisible government, which is the true ruling power of our country."*

Let that sink in. Propaganda isn't just about ads or campaign slogans. It's about control. And it's practiced by every central power circle on Earth.

The Four Marks of Propaganda

To know propaganda, you must spot its traits. Here's what makes something propaganda:

1. **It's persuasive –** It's trying to move you.
2. **It represents someone's agenda –** Someone benefits.
3. **It has a factual or logical flaw –** Something is wrong or omitted.
4. **It creates a strong emotional response –** e.g., Fear, anger, guilt, pride.

If you spot all four? You're looking at propaganda.

The Belief Pyramid

Propaganda aims at your beliefs, not your intellect. Why? Because beliefs drive thoughts, thoughts drive feelings, and feelings drive action. That's the traditional view.

The modern view? We make emotional decisions and use logic *after the fact* to justify them. Either way, beliefs are the base layer. And propaganda wants in.

The Five Pillars of Belief

Why do we believe what we believe? Here's the structure—based on insights from One Idea to Rule Them All[6] by Michelle Stiles (pulling from Le Bon's work[7]):

1. **Authority –** You trust the guy in the lab coat.
2. **Experience –** You've seen it, so you believe it.
3. **Social Pressure –** You go along to get along.
4. **Imagination –** You believe stories, even ones you've never seen.
5. **Language –** Words shape thoughts, and thoughts shape actions.

6 Michelle Stiles, One Idea to Rule Them All: Reverse Engineering American Propaganda, Kindle ed. (November 29, 2022), 268 pages.
7 Gustave Le Bon, The Crowd: A Study of the Popular Mind (December 24, 2016; reprint edition), 138 pages, ISBN 1636000169.

Let's break those down with examples:

- **Authority:** You brush your teeth because a dentist said so. You believe in cells because a biology teacher told you (not because you've seen mitosis).
- **Experience:** You believe football is better than basketball because you've played both.
- **Social Pressure:** Remember the early COVID-19 pandemic news? The official origin story was that the virus came from a 'wet market' in China? If anyone even questioned it, they could feel the ridicule. That's pressure.
- **Imagination:** Maybe you never saw your grandpa picking cotton without electricity, but he told the story, and now your mind's eye plays it like a movie. That image fuels your drive.

- **Language:** If I tell a new police trainee to "kill the threat," they might balk. But if I say "neutralize the threat" over and over, it gets internalized more easily since 'neutralize' is a more 'morally palatable' word. We often underrate the power of language.

Types of Propaganda

Now that we know *what* propaganda is and *how* it works, let's look at the different kinds[8]:

- **White Propaganda –** Open source. You know who's talking. It's biased, but honest about the source.
- **Gray Propaganda –** Murky source. Think "anonymous officials say..." It's unclear where the message is coming from.
- **Black Propaganda –** Flat-out lies. Disguised origin. Example: Germany attacks Russia but blames China using fake cyber sources. It's all deception, all the way down.

These terms date back to World War II and are still used in modern psychological operations and media strategies.

Why This Matters

Now that you know what propaganda is, what it's made of, and how it penetrates belief systems, you're already less vulnerable. Like understanding how a bullet works, you're better equipped to build armor that stops it.

Let's keep building that shield.

8 Daniel Lerner, Psychological Warfare Against Nazi Germany: The Skyewar Campaign, D-Day to VE-Day (Cambridge, MA: MIT Press, 1971), 432 pages.

CHAPTER 4:
The Barrel: How Propaganda Gets Delivered

We've covered what propaganda is, what it does, and why it's dangerous. If propaganda is the bullet, this chapter is about the *barrel*—the delivery system that fires it into your heart and mind.

It's not enough to understand the damage. We need to understand the path—the route from idea to impact. And once you see how it works, you won't unsee it.

From Thought to Target: Delivery Systems Explained

Just like a bullet needs a barrel to reach a target, propaganda needs a mechanism to reach your heart and mind. And just like with a bullet, the damage is already underway once it enters.

A Historical Blueprint: The CPI

Let's rewind to 1917. President Woodrow Wilson ran for office, promising to keep the U.S. out of World War I. Then he broke that promise. The public didn't want war, but elements of the political class did.

Enter the **Committee on Public Information (CPI)**[9]: America's first formal, federal propaganda agency. Wilson didn't rely on logic or transparency. He built a media machine that targeted the belief pillars we outlined in the previous chapter.

The CPI had eight divisions. Let's walk through them:

---

9 George Creel, How We Advertised America: The First Telling of the Amazing Story of the Committee on Public Information That Carried the Gospel of Americanism to Every Corner of the Globe (Forgotten Books, 2018),

1. Domestic News Division

Popularized Ivy Lee's concept of the "press release." Instead of reporters chasing facts, they were handed bullet points straight from the government. Sound familiar?

2. Foreign News Division

Similar to the above, but tailored for international audiences. Exporting the narrative abroad.

3. Advertising Division

Controlled billboard space and print ads. The CPI reps would work deals with the billboard owners and newspapers: "Are you a patriot or not?" Patriotism was the pressure point used to co-opt ad space.

4. Division of Pictorial Publicity

Recruited artists and cartoonists. Their job? Visually stir fear, rage, and loyalty. CPI officials had a way of pressuring these artists. Imagine a German boot stomping a baby. The artists did.

5. Division of Films

This was the Hollywood pipeline before Hollywood existed. The government commissioned films with pro-war messages.

6. Division of Speaking

The CPI recruited respected local figures—pastors, businesspeople, and community leaders—and provided them with talking points to use in their discussions. They gave speeches at community events and even in the middle of movie reel changes. These people were known as **the Four Minute Men**.

7. Youth Public Speaking Division

Yes, they had kids doing it too. Junior Four Minute Men delivered pre-written messages in schools. Propaganda became an extracurricular activity.

8. National School Service Bulletin

This was the federal Trojan horse into education. Teachers received mandatory talking points, reading prompts, and essay assignments. "Imagine you are an innocent European being stomped by the Kaiser..." Students wrote essays reinforcing propaganda themes. (If you assigned a reading or writing assignment that hypothetically advocates for a political position ... you're more likely to adopt that position!).[10]

A Surround Sound Psy-Op

What does this all add up to?

Not just messaging. Saturation.

The CPI filled every space—billboards, movies, schools, churches, even dinner conversations—with a coordinated campaign to shape how you felt, thought, and behaved.

This was before smartphones. Before TV. Before 24/7 feeds.

Now? Multiply that delivery system by the power of AI, digital media, and algorithmic targeting.

You're not just hearing propaganda. You're swimming in it.

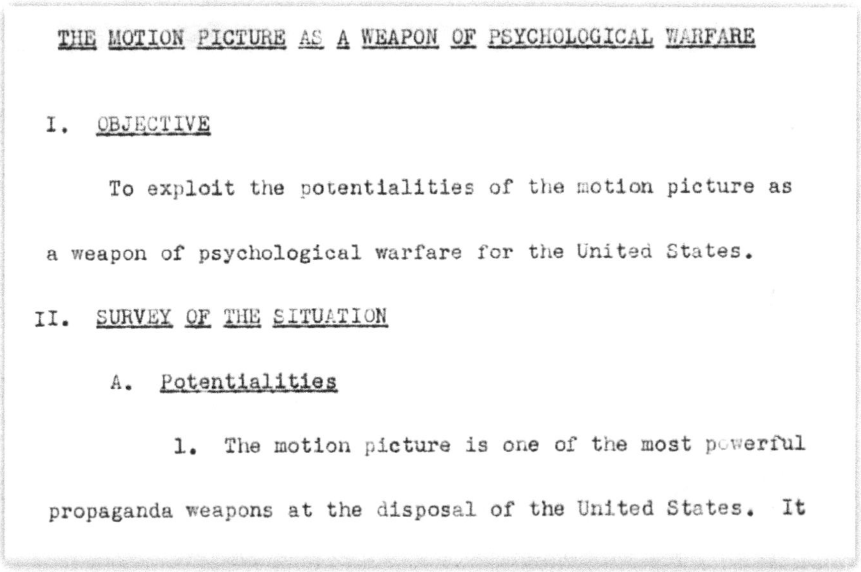

THE MOTION PICTURE AS A WEAPON OF PSYCHOLOGICAL WARFARE

I. OBJECTIVE

To exploit the potentialities of the motion picture as a weapon of psychological warfare for the United States.

II. SURVEY OF THE SITUATION

A. Potentialities

1. The motion picture is one of the most powerful propaganda weapons at the disposal of the United States. It

A Declassified 1943 OSS Memo Emphasizing the Importance of Propaganda in Movies[11]

10 N. Schwarz, D. Frey, and M. Kumpf, *"Interactive Effects of Writing and Reading a Persuasive Essay on Attitude Change and Selective Exposure," Journal of Experimental Social Psychology* 16 (1980): 1–17,

11 **Office of Strategic Services**. *The Motion Picture as a Weapon of Psychological Warfare*. Washington, D.C., 1943. Declassified 2004. Available via National Archives and referenced at Clandestine Services Archive

Why It Matters

You can't block the bullet if you don't see the barrel. You can't build a shield for your kids if you don't understand the weaponry.

Understanding the CPI model helps you identify its modern equivalents. We will hammer the modern 'heart and mind' landscape in the last chapter of this book.

Now that you know how the CPI delivered analogue propaganda, you're ready to begin identifying its presence everywhere in its digital forms.

Let's keep strengthening that shield.

CHAPTER 5:
The Wizard's Pitch: How Propaganda Sells Without Selling

Imagine being a struggling salesperson, grinding 60 hours a week. Then a genie appears and says, "You'll never have to chase customers again. They'll come to you—begging to buy."

Sound impossible?

Welcome to the magic of propaganda.

In this chapter, we move from government manipulation to commercial persuasion. The exact mechanics apply—only the product changes. Let's break it down.

Enter Bernays, the Wizard of the Market

Edward Bernays—yes, the same guy who doubled cigarette sales to women and helped America embrace WWI in the CPI—once shared how he'd sell something as commercially 'elastic' as a piano.

He didn't go door to door. He didn't run a discount ad.

Instead, he constructed a surround-sound narrative. It would look something like this.

- He called friends at the major newspapers to write a piece about how upper-class homes now had piano parlors.
- He tapped a **doctor** to write in the health section about the calming benefits of piano music.
- He got **housekeeping magazines** to publish stories about how model homemakers would find peace in the tranquility of piano music.

- He had an **architectural magazine** talk about how the newest designs were building entire rooms around pianos.

Do you see it?

By the time the average reader encountered the piano ad, they weren't being sold anything. Bernays used his sock puppet intermediaries to show what was normal, high-status, and even healthy.

Customers began to pursue the goods and services. Many of the salespeople in Bernay's domains became order-takers.

How It Works: Agenda Wrapped in Appeal

This is the trick: **You don't sell your agenda directly. You wrap it in something the target already wants.**

Take the three examples we've covered:

1. **Cigarettes for Women** – The sale wasn't "Buy smokes." It was "Assert your independence."
2. **WWI for the U.S.** – The slogan wasn't "Send your sons to die." It was "Protect democracy."
3. **Pianos for Everyone** – The sale wasn't "Buy this expensive instrument." It was "Everyone cool and successful has a piano parlor."

The goal is always the same: Find the soft spot. Press it. Wrap your motive in the target's desire.

Propaganda Today: Same Trick, More Firepower

This isn't dusty history. It's today's marketing playbook—and today's geopolitics.

Take this example: In 2010, WikiLeaks exposed a CIA memo. It revealed concerns that France and Germany might withdraw from **Afghanistan**.[12]

The solution?

- **For France:** Emphasize the humanitarian crisis and the plight of female refugees.

12 Central Intelligence Agency, *CIA Report into Shoring Up Afghan War Support in Western Europe*, March 11, 2010, published by WikiLeaks on March 26, 2010, https://wikileaks.org/wiki/CIA_red_cell_memo_shoring_up_Afghan_war_support.

- **For Germany:** Highlight concerns about heroin trafficking and mass migration.

The strategy: **Press different buttons in different cultures.**

This is *textbook propaganda*, applied at scale by intelligence agencies and/or their public relations contractors. It's what the large modern PR firms do every day—from soda sales to social engineering.

What You're Seeing Is a Hall of Mirrors

Bernays' piano playbook didn't die with the Jazz Age. It evolved. Now, you see it in social media influencers, pseudo-expert blog posts, viral reels, and TikTok videos...and "scientific" articles funded by interested parties.

The result?

We live in a hall of mirrors. We don't just question *what* we're seeing—we forget to question *why* we're seeing it at all.

That's the game. That's the trick.

Where We're Headed Next

This chapter completes the core framework of your shield. You now understand:

- What propaganda is
- How it affects beliefs
- How it's delivered
- How it disguises itself to get inside your heart and mind

We're almost ready to examine propaganda's arsenal—the actual techniques. These are the tools used by governments, brands, influencers, and sometimes even by us or our friends, often without anyone realizing it.

First, let's cover a couple of important questions before we dive into the meat of the techniques.

CHAPTER 6:
The Moral Question: Is Propaganda Always Evil?

Here's an uncomfortable truth: if you put 10 thoughtful people in a room and ask whether propaganda is moral, you'll likely get 10 different answers. That's because propaganda isn't just one thing. It's a tool, like a scalpel or a sword, depending on who's holding it.

Let's talk about morality, manipulation, and how to prepare yourself for the rest of the book.

Bernays' Justification: The Elite Must Rule the Narrative

Edward Bernays, the father of modern propaganda, had no illusions about democracy. He didn't believe that most citizens were equipped to understand complex international or political issues. Therefore, in his view, the "intelligent minority" (read: elites in New York and Washington) had a moral obligation to guide the public via propaganda.

Roughly speaking, his vision of 'democracy' was daddy gripping the wheel, steering the whims of the populace.

Local vs National: A Moral Framework

Now contrast Bernays' top-down pyramid with what America's founders envisioned: **federalism**—a bottom-up structure of distributed authority.

1. **The individual** holds the most authority
2. Some of that authority is entrusted to the **family**
3. Some of the family authority is entrusted to the **local community**

4. Some of the community authority is entrusted to the US **state**
5. And finally, the US states would entrust some of their fate to the **national government**, which was designed to hold the *least* authority in most matters

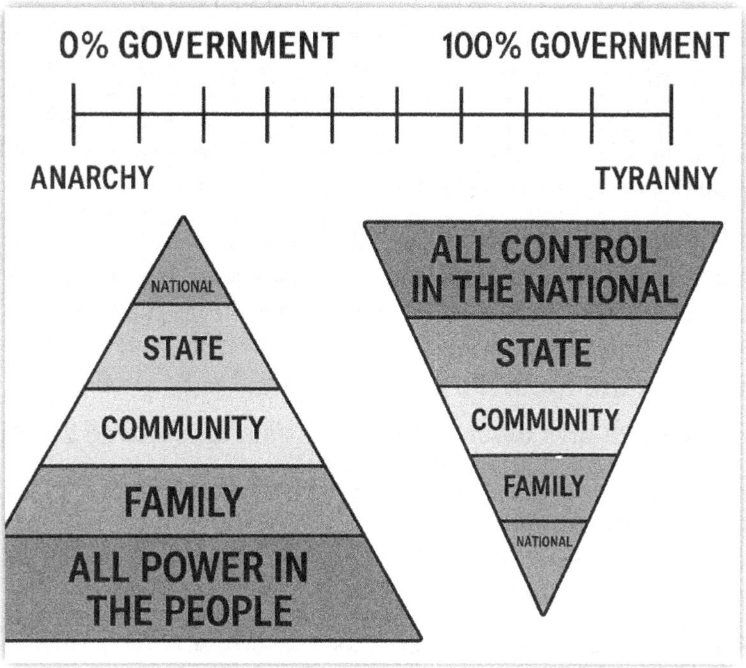

Let's bring it down to earth.

- When a **parent** tells a kid, "Eat your spinach ...it makes you strong," that's propaganda-ish. It's vague and agenda-driven, but done with the child's good in mind.
- A **football coach** yelling "Pain is weakness leaving the body!" to his players is propaganda-ish, too ...but aimed at team cohesion and growth.

In local settings with mutual buy-in and accountability, propaganda is often just part of *culture-building*.

But when it's deployed **nationally**, top-down, with no room for exit or dissent? That's something else.

At that level, if you're a believer in limited government or individual sovereignty, it feels less like persuasion and more like coercion.

That's one lens I use to judge propaganda: *Where is it coming from? Who does it benefit? Can the recipient walk away?*

Persuasion vs Manipulation

Here's another critical distinction we must address before moving further:

- **Persuasion** aims to help the listener. "Eat your spinach—it'll help you grow." The person persuading believes it's in your best interest.
- **Manipulation** exploits the listener. Imagine if spinach were known to harm people, but I promoted it anyway because a company paid me to do so. Now I'm deceiving you for *my* benefit, at your expense.

Manipulation is persuasion that exploits.

Our goal in this book is clear: **Fight exploitation**. Recognize persuasion. Get smarter than the con artists and their messaging.

How to Get the Most Out of This Book

Now that we've built the framework, it's time to reinforce the shield.

Here's how:

1. **Review the chapters** – If anything didn't stick, go back. Actively look for examples of these methods in the 'wild' as you learn. This will tune your brain to learn much faster.
2. **Pretend you have to teach this tomorrow** – One of the best ways to learn is to learn as if you'll have to explain it to someone else.
3. **Engage with the materials** – Video lectures available at propagandashield.com (as a book buyer, you get discounted access if you want to take your learning process to the next level)
4. **Talk about this stuff** – With your spouse, your kids, your neighbors. Propaganda touches everything. The more you discuss it, the easier it becomes to spot.

There's a certain beauty to these discussions due to the revealing nature of them. Why do you believe what you believe? Who shaped that belief? Is there a Devil Dave whispering in your ear?

Let's find out.

Next up: The classic techniques—many are straight from the Institute for Propaganda Analysis and beyond.

Let's go.

SECTION II - THE FUNDAMENTAL PROPAGANDA TECHNIQUES

CHAPTER 7: OVERVIEW: The Techniques: Fallacies That Bypass Your Brain

Congratulations. If you've made it this far, you've built the foundation. You now understand what propaganda is, how it works, how it's delivered, and how it disguises itself as something you want.

Now it's time to learn how to recognize it in the wild.

Welcome to the **rhetorical technique** section of the book—the most common fallacies, errors, and psychological sleights-of-hand used to bypass the rational brain. This is the part you will love because you'll soon be spotting these fallacies everywhere.

Why This Matters

The techniques you're about to learn are not theoretical. You see them every day—on your phone, on billboards, in classrooms, even in casual conversations. They're designed to *bypass logic* and go straight to your emotions.

And the best defense? **Recognition, then taking the message to court (so to speak)**

The moment you can name the technique the messenger is using, its power starts to fade... especially if you've started with the 'N-E' of NESTPAD.

Yes, there's more to modern propaganda than logical fallacies—like coercion, censorship, and algorithmic control (more on this in the last section of the book)—but this is the bedrock. These are the fundamentals. Learn them now, and you'll have them for life.

A Word of Caution

Not every fallacy is propaganda. Sometimes people are just talking.

If your buddy says, "The Springfield Lions are the best baseball team ever," that's not necessarily propaganda. That's just a guy talking smack. Especially for younger learners, be cautious not to become overly enthusiastic about this subject. Don't let yourself or your kid become the guy interrupting every conversation to label fallacies in friendly banter.

The goal here is to learn how to identify **persuasive messages aimed at shaping belief or behavior**, not to become the fallacy police at lunch.

Where We're Starting

We're beginning with some classic techniques from the **Institute for Propaganda Analysis (IPA)**. But that's just the start. This course will cover the most common methods that PR firms and political movements use daily. These are the real-world tools of influence and emotional manipulation.

We will pair each technique with practical examples, and the list of techniques will expand over time in our e-course as new ones emerge.

A Key Definition Refined

A core element of our working definition of propaganda is that it involves:

"Errors or omissions in facts or logic."

We're borrowing and adapting this concept from debate literature, particularly John T. Reed's *How to Spot Dishonest Arguments*.[13] His work focuses on dishonest debate tactics (finding error or omission in your opponent's facts or logic), but the overlap with propaganda is enormous.

So, here's the slight shift: **Your job in defending yourself against propaganda is finding an error or omission in your messenger's facts or logic.**

13 John T. Reed, *How to Spot Dishonest Arguments and Keep Your Own Thinking Straight* (John T. Reed Publishing, n.d.), 119 pages.

A Fallacy Doesn't Mean It's False

Just because a message uses a fallacy doesn't mean the message itself is untrue. It just means you should **scrutinize the message**.. Please take it to court.

The goal is not to reject without thought, but to investigate.

Your Mnemonic Weapon: NESTPAD

Every time you're exposed to a persuasive message, run it through this quick process:

- **N**ame the **E**motion it provokes in you.
- **S**ay the **T**echnique that you just witnessed.
- **P**rove the message (Can you back it up with supporting evidence?)
- **A**nd
- **D**isprove the message (Can you challenge it with supporting evidence?)

That's **NESTPAD**.

If you make this mental algorithm second nature, you'll become more propaganda-resistant in every situation. And better yet, you'll be able to teach your loved ones how to do the same.

Let's get into the techniques. This is where your shield gets bulletproof...

CHAPTER 8:
Appeal to Emotion: The First and Most Powerful Trick

If you've ever tried to learn a new language, you know you can't just jump into sentences without first learning the alphabet. That's what many of these initial technique chapters are: the emotional alphabet of propaganda. And the first "letter" we need to master is the **Appeal to Emotion**.

This is the bedrock technique—woven into almost every other. It's also the most potent.

What Is Appeal to Emotion?

It's when someone sends a message designed to stir your emotions **without backing it with solid facts or logic**.

Example: "Don't go swimming in the ocean, you'll get eaten by a shark."

- **Fact check?** Missing.
- **Emotional impact?** Immediate.

Same thing in advertising: "If you don't buy this book, you'll end up broke."

Or politics: "If you vote for my opponent, nuclear war is inevitable."

Fear is the most common trigger. But it's not the only one. Messengers often use guilt, shame, pride, anger, sadness, and hope to convey their messages.

Not All Emotional Appeals Are Evil

People often truly believe what they're saying. Emotion alone doesn't make a message manipulative, but it does mean the message deserves to be **put on trial**.

For example, my message: "If we don't help our children resist harmful messaging, they might get crushed by it."

That's emotional. But it could also be true. So, please take it to court. Don't reject it outright, but don't swallow it whole either.

Classic Emotional Propaganda Example: LBJ's "Daisy Ad"

In 1964, President Lyndon B. Johnson's campaign aired a famous political ad:

A little girl counts petals. A mushroom cloud explodes. Voiceover: "These are the stakes... We must either love each other, or we must die."

The message? If you don't vote for Johnson, you might die in a nuclear war.

That's pure appeal to emotion.

Where It Comes From

Modern emotional propaganda is rooted in psychological research, especially *Maslow's hierarchy of needs*. PR consultants figured out that you can manipulate people by appealing to their needs for:

- **Love**
- **Prosperity**
- **Immortality**

Or by threatening them with:

- **Rejection**
- **Powerlessness**
- **Death**

APPEAL TO EMOTION

DESIRE FOR	FEAR OF
love	rejection
prosperity	powerlessness
immortality	death

Frozen Doom: When Science Sold Helplessness

On July 9, 1971, *The Washington Post* ran a headline warning that:

"The world could be as little as 50 or 60 years away from a new ice age, a leading atmospheric scientist predicts."

The article is a prime example of a fear based article, using the specter of an unstoppable global catastrophe to instill a sense of helplessness. By placing the supposed disaster within a single human lifetime, it amplified urgency and dread, not to spark individual action, but to breed reliance on experts and institutions. The unspoken message was clear: *you're powerless to stop it, but trust us, and maybe we can.*

Visuals Hit Harder

Images + emotions = supercharged propaganda.

Take this WWII poster: terrifying enemy figures threatening your home, wife, and child. The message? "Buy war bonds—or this will happen to you."

WARNING!
OUR HOMES ARE IN DANGER NOW!
OUR JOB
KEEP 'EM FIRING

How to Fight It: NESTPAD

Let's use our defensive technique:

- **N**ame the **E**motion: FEAR
- **Say** the **T**echnique: "This is an appeal to fear."
- **P**rove the message: Is there evidence that this message is valid?
- **A**nd
- **Disprove** the message: Is there evidence that this is hype and exaggeration?

Fight Confirmation Bias With The 'PAD' of NESTPAD

Let's say someone says, "Sharks will eat you if you go swimming in Florida."

You Google "shark attacks in Florida" ...you'll find headlines. Lots of them. It *feels* convincing.

But now, search "low odds of shark attack in Florida."

Very low. Probably lower than being struck by lightning.

That second search is vital ('disproving the message'). It kills confirmation bias, which is the tendency to only look at information that squares up with your existing beliefs. If you have the integrity to genuinely pursue the truth, this step is VITAL. Read that sentence again.

Once you reach the 'PAD' stage of NESTPAD, you've moved past the emotional part of the message, and now you're the jury. To keep your thinking clear and balanced, you MUST listen to both the 'prosecution' and the 'defense'.

Case Study: Appeal to Emotion

NESTPAD Application for Case Study

- **N**ame the **E**motion: FEAR
- **Say** the **T**echnique: "This is an appeal to emotion."
- **P**rove the message: Let's follow the facts and logic that we'll lose our democracy if she gets elected.
- And
- **Disprove** the message: Compile evidence that she's a fierce **defender** of democracy

Final Note: Facts Plus Emotion = Credibility

If a message triggers emotion but also brings solid evidence, give it some credit. That doesn't mean you unquestioningly trust it—but it does mean it's worth a deeper look.

Key Takeaways:

- Appeal to emotion is the foundation of most propaganda.
- It plays on your deepest fears and desires.
- Use facts and logic when your emotions are tripped.

And now, you've got a tool to beat it: **NESTPAD**.

Next up, we'll explore another common trick that slips past logic when no one's looking.

You're moving along well. Let's keep moving forward.

CHAPTER 9:
Proof by Assertion

Have you ever noticed how something starts to sound true after hearing it enough times? That's not an accident. It's a psychological trick called **the illusory truth effect**, and its main ingredient is **proof by assertion**, and it's one of the most common (and dangerous) propaganda tools out there.

What Is Proof by Assertion?

It's when someone **states a debatable opinion or claim as if it's a fact**.

If you hear a debatable opinion or claim as fact often enough, you'll probably eventually accept it.

Examples of 'Proof by Assertion' in the Wild

In conversation:

- "The Springfield Rockets are the best team ever."

In advertising:

- "Home of the world's greatest cup of coffee." (Elf fans, we see you.)

In politics:

- "My opponent hates poor people."

All of these are **assertions**, stated as **facts**, designed to slip past your brain and into your belief system.

Why It Works: The Illusory Truth Effect

This is real psychology: **The more often you hear a claim, the more likely you are to believe it[14]**. The philosophical label for this assertion style is 'argumentum ad nauseam.'

Sometimes it only takes three repetitions for your brain to start accepting a statement as accurate, especially if those repeating the assertion say it confidently and are in positions that give them credibility. That's why propaganda campaigns hammer slogans, taglines, and talking points over and over.

Circular and Unfalsifiable Assertions

Some assertions double back on themselves (circular assertions):

> "This product works great because it has amazing health benefits."
>
> "How do you know it has health benefits?"
>
> "Because it works great."

There are other assertions that you can't prove to be false (unfalsifiable assertions):

- "John Doe only thinks about himself."
- "Experts say that among the 50k bales of hay in Kansas, not one of them contains any lint."
- "Anonymous sources say John Doe wet himself in a meeting."

There's no way to disprove these. That's why they're powerful.

This overlaps with gray and black propaganda, where anonymous sources and unverifiable claims are used to erode trust or destroy reputations. As a rule, it's best to put low credibility ratings on stories with 'anonymous' sources. Propagandists love these 'unfalsifiable' assertions if they support their narrative.

Scott Adams' Rule: Mind Reading Isn't Real

Take that example: "John Doe only thinks about himself." Propaganda enthusiast, Scott Adams (creator of Dilbert), calls this for what it is: mind reading.

---

14 Jessica Udry and Sarah J. Barber, *"The Illusory Truth Effect: A Review of How Repetition Increases Belief in Misinformation,"* Current Opinion in Psychology 56 (April 2024): 101736, https://doi.org/10.1016/j.copsyc.2023.101736.

News headlines and political messages often suggest to you what someone else is thinking, why they did something, or what their *real* motives were. But unless they're psychic... they're just asserting.

Popularity ≠ Truth

Another common tactic is the **appeal to popular assertion**:

▶ "Everyone knows you need to drink eight glasses of water a day."

You've probably heard that your whole life. But is it true?

Maybe. But you won't know unless you take it to court.

The Advertiser's Edge

Take this real ad:

"America's favorite mascara."

It *sounds* impressive. But can you disprove that claim? How would you even begin? That's why it's effective.

Ad writers know how to thread that needle. They're bold enough to persuade, vague enough to avoid scrutiny.

Case Study: Assertion as Fact

NESTPAD Application for Case Study

- **N**ame the **E**motion: Resentment, Moral Superiority
- **S**ay the **T**echnique: "This is an assertion stated as fact."
- **P**rove the message: 'Let's find supporting evidence that he left because of "embarrassment."
- And
- **Disprove** the message: 'Let's find supporting evidence that he left for a different reason.'

Another Example:

> *"Everyone needs eight glasses of water a day."*

- Emotion: None.
- Technique: Proof by popular assertion.
- Prove: Search for health sources supporting the claim.
- Disprove: Search for "8 glass water myth" or "debunked hydration rule."

Again, this last step—**trying to disprove the message**—is what makes you immune to **confirmation bias**. Confirmation bias is a death spiral to your maturity (you only look at information that agrees with your foregone conclusions). It's likely the #1 thing that keeps us human beings from maturing. Truth will stand on its own at the end of the day. It doesn't need your help. It only asks for your honest pursuit of it.

Final Tip: Reward Honesty

Give extra credibility to communicators who **distinguish fact from opinion.**

If someone says:

> *"To be clear, this next point is just my speculation..."*

That's a good sign. It shows they (at minimum) care about their credibility. And it helps you trust that they're not trying to slip something past you.

Key Takeaways:

- Assertion is the most common propaganda technique.
- It typically relies on repetition and your tendency to trust the familiar.
- Circular logic, unfalsifiable claims, and appeals to popularity are all variations.
- Use NESTPAD to expose and defeat it.

You're now one step closer to becoming propaganda-proof. Next up: another technique that hides in plain sight.

CHAPTER 10: Bandwagon: Why Everyone's Doing It (and Why That Shouldn't Matter)

There's an old parenting cliché that goes something like this:

> *"If little Johnny jumped off a bridge, would you do it too?"*

Most kids have heard it. Most parents have said it. And most of us, at some point, rolled our eyes and shrugged it off.

But modern psychology says... yes. Yes you would jump off a bridge if enough people were jumping with Johnny.

That's not sarcasm. That's the reality of human behavior. Our natural, deeply embedded drive to fit in, to stay safe in the group, to belong; it's wired into our psychology. And it makes us vulnerable.

This lesson is about one of the most potent and consistent techniques in the propagandist's toolbox: **Bandwagoning**.

"Everybody's Doing It" — The Ancient Trick

Let's start with a quote from Edward Bernays:

> *"He buys a car because it is, at the moment, the group custom to buy cars."*

Not because he needs it. Not because it's the right financial decision. But because *that's what everyone is doing.*

Now let's throw in some psychological firepower. The **Asch Conformity Experiment**[15] is a legendary study in which psychologists asked a participant to pick the length of a line. Easy, right? Only one catch: everyone else in the room was an actor, and they intentionally chose the wrong answer. The real participant, just one person, usually folded. Even when the answer was blatantly wrong, he went along with the group.

Why?

Because we are social creatures, and the idea of standing alone is scarier than being wrong for most of us.

What Is Bandwagoning?

Bandwagoning is the act of validating an idea, product, or person by pointing to their popularity.

It doesn't matter if the thing is true. It doesn't matter if the idea is good. The whole point is this:

> *"If lots of people believe it, it must be true."*

Here's how it sounds in the wild:

- **In conversation:** "How can you hate *Avatar*? It's the highest-grossing movie of all time."
- **In advertising:** "This is the best-selling electric car in the USA."
- **In politics:** "95% of social scientists agree that spanking your kids will backfire."

See the pattern? You're being pushed to go along, not by logic, but by popularity.

Why Bandwagoning Works

It hijacks two of your most sensitive psychological triggers:

- The **fear of rejection**
- The **desire for prosperity and belonging**

---

15 Solomon E. Asch, "Studies of Independence and Conformity: I. A Minority of One Against a Unanimous Majority," *Psychological Monographs: General and Applied* 70, no. 9 (1956): 1–70, https://doi.org/10.1037/h0093718.

And here's the kicker: bandwagon doesn't usually show up alone. It runs with a crew. It often teams up with **appeal to authority** (more on this later) and assertion to form a deadly trio of persuasive manipulation.

"But What If It's True?"

It might be.

Let's be clear: **many popular ideas are true.**

But their **truth is independent of their popularity.**

And that's what we want you (and your loved ones) to learn. Just because a lot of people believe something doesn't mean it's true. And just because something is true doesn't mean everyone will accept it.

Classic Example: World War I Propaganda

Message: "Every Man in Uniform Is Doing His Duty. Why Aren't You?"

That's not a suggestion. That's a moral gut-punch. It's pure bandwagon. Everyone's doing it. The implication? You're a coward if you don't.

It worked back then. It still works today.

Case Study: Bandwagon

NESTPAD Application for Case Study

Name the Emotion:

Loss of Confidence, Self-Doubt, Fear of Isolation

Say the Technique:

'This looks like it could be a bandwagon technique.'

Prove the message:

'Let's evaluate the strength of the spanking study.'

And

Disprove the message:

Find authoritative sources that contradict the spanking study.

Key Takeaways:

- Bandwagon appeals to popularity, not logic.
- It's effective because it exploits our social wiring.
- Truth and popularity are not the same thing.
- You can fight back by using the NESTPAD method: identify the emotion, spot the technique, and evaluate both sides.

Let's Keep Moving Forward. You're already miles ahead of where you used to be.

CHAPTER 11:
The Spotlight Fallacy: What You See Isn't Always What Matters

You've probably heard the phrase:

> *"Out of sight, out of mind."*

But the inverse is just as powerful:

> *"In sight, in mind."*

This lesson might be the most subtly dangerous yet, because it has nothing to do with logic, argumentation, or even persuasion in the traditional sense. It bypasses all that. It plays with your attention.

Welcome to **Agenda Setting Theory**—the concept that whatever 'the media' focuses on is perceived as important.

Note: *The term Spotlight Fallacy sometimes refers to the mistaken belief that others are paying more attention to us than they are. However, we use it as a catchy nickname for the availability bias since it captures the idea so well.*

It's not always what's being said. It's how often it's being said. How frequently. How loudly. And how widely.

What Is the Spotlight Fallacy?

At its core, what we're calling the spotlight fallacy is this:

> *"People conclude something is important based on how much the media covers it."*

This is dangerous because it operates beneath the level of critical thinking. You're not being persuaded — you're being **primed**. If a story is in your face every day, it starts to live rent-free in your head. And if the media chooses what's in your face... well, they're choosing what fills your mind.

This is not a matter of left versus right. This is a *human cognition* thing. It applies to everyone.

Shark Attacks and Affairs

Let's say the news spends two weeks running breathless stories about shark attacks. You're not on the beach. You've never been attacked. You don't even know anyone who has. But suddenly, a buddy invites you to Destin, FL — and your brain flashes **"shark".** That's not logic. That's availability bias steering your thoughts and decisions.

Or let's say a senator's alleged affair dominates headlines for 90 days. No new evidence. No trial. Just constant coverage. Eventually, the subconscious assumption becomes:

"If it's on the news this much, it must be true."

That's how this fallacy works. It doesn't argue. It drowns out alternatives.

Why It Matters More Than Ever

The spotlight fallacy is more dangerous today than ever before, because:

1. **Legacy media is struggling**, which means they chase sensationalism to survive.
2. **Clickbait rules the algorithms**. More outrageous = more engagement.
3. **Governments, activists, and PR firms all know how to exploit the media's hunger for attention.**

You've heard of media stunts? That's this.

Books like *Beautiful Trouble*[16] and *Trust Me, I'm Lying*[17] (a media manipulator's handbook) both teach how to **engineer the spotlight**. Not by truth. Not by substance. By spectacle. By technique.

And it works. Throw red paint on a fur coat. Get arrested on purpose. Plant a story in a small blog and let it ripple upward until CNN bites. It's not about **what's true**. It's about **what gets seen**.

How to Protect Your Mind: The Spotlight Filter

You can't out-debate the spotlight fallacy. It's not about logic. It's about attention. What gets repeated gets remembered. What stays in view starts to feel important, even if it's not.

The only surefire way to protect yourself from the spotlight fallacy is also the most impractical: avoid media entirely. We all know ... sometimes you *can't* just unplug. You might be in school. You might need to follow the news for your job. So, what do you do?

Use the Spotlight Filter. Inspired by Rabbi Daniel Lapin, this tool helps you guard your mental real estate, even when you're surrounded by noise.[18]

Ask one question:

Does this 'message' impact one of my '5 Fs?'

- Faith
- Family
- Friendships
- Finances
- Fitness

If it does, pay attention. Run the message through NESTPAD. If it doesn't — file it, filter it, or forget it.

You don't have to ignore everything (nor can you). Just prioritize ruthlessly. Your attention is precious. Guard it like your life depends on it, because your peace of mind does.

---

16 Andrew Boyd and Dave Oswald Mitchell, *Beautiful Trouble: A Toolbox for Revolution* (New York: OR Books, 2016), 474 pages.

17 Ryan Holiday, *Trust Me, I'm Lying: Confessions of a Media Manipulator*, 5th anniversary ed. (New York: Portfolio, 2013), 352 pages.

18 Daniel Lapin and Susan Lapin, *The Holistic You: Integrating Your Family, Finances, Faith, Friendships, and Fitness* (Hoboken, NJ: Wiley, 2023), 272 pages.

Key Takeaways – Chapter 11: The Spotlight Fallacy

- The spotlight fallacy tricks you into thinking something is important just because it's constantly covered.
- It bypasses logic and uses repetition to prime your attention and shape your perception.
- Modern media thrives on sensationalism, making this bias more potent than ever.
- The danger isn't in what's said — it's in how often and how loudly it's said.
- Use the Spotlight Filter: focus only on messages that affect your Faith, Family, Friendships, Finances, or Fitness.

Your mind is getting sharper by the minute. Keep moving forward!

CHAPTER 12:
Appeal to Authority

Have you ever heard of something called **Gell-Mann Amnesia**? It's funny—and terrifying.

Physicist **Murray Gell-Mann** described the experience of reading a newspaper article on a topic he knew intimately, like physics, and realizing the journalist got it completely wrong. Not just off by a little. Entirely backwards. He'd shake his head, frustrated at the inaccuracy...

Then turn the page and read another article on foreign policy or economics, and accept it at face value.

That's **Gell-Mann Amnesia**: if the media botches the story you know, why unquestioningly trust the ones you don't?

Many veterans know this feeling. They've lived through combat, seen the chaos up close, then watched the media's version of events and thought, *"Were we even in the same war?"*

Now here's where this ties into propaganda:

Appeal to authority works best *when Gell-Mann Amnesia kicks in.* We forget how often the so-called experts get things wrong, so we unquestioningly trust them the next time they speak.

What Is an Appeal to Authority?

An **appeal to authority** is a rhetorical move where a debatable claim is accepted as fact simply because it was made by someone with credentials or a title, or a news source of 'a stellar reputation'.

Yes, real experts matter. Engineers, scientists, doctors; we owe them plenty. But propaganda doesn't rely on actual wisdom.

It thrives by **abusing the label or suggestion of "authority"** to silence questions and shut down debate.

So, the danger isn't in expertise itself. The danger is when **the illusion of expertise** becomes a weapon.

Examples

In Conversation:

- "We need to adopt this economic policy. Dr. Richard Johnson, who has a PhD in economics from Harvard, says it's essential."
- Credentials aren't a substitute for evidence. If the argument holds water, it should stand up to scrutiny—**even from someone without a degree.**

In Advertising:

- "Drink this magnesium supplement—Taylor Swift takes it."
- Taylor might be brilliant at making popular music that sells, but that doesn't make her a medical expert. This is **misapplied credibility**—classic appeal to authority with a sprinkle of celebrity worship.

In Politics:

- "Dozens of retired generals say this bill will save democracy."
- Maybe it will. But unless those generals lay out the **why**, their titles alone shouldn't silence debate. Consensus without proof is just **well-dressed groupthink**.

Bottom line:

An appeal to authority becomes propaganda when it bypasses your brain. **If someone can't defend their position without hiding behind a title, it's not a strong position.**

Case Study: Appeal to Authority

Case Study: NESTPAD

Name the Emotion

Fear of being wrong. Respect for intellect. Intimidated from going against the 'official narrative.'

Say the Technique

Appeal to Authority.

Prove the Claim

Ask: Can the authority back up their assertion that the Earth is flat? Check their credentials, their track record, and their supporting evidence.

And Disprove the Claim

Look for credible experts who disagree that the Earth is flat. Read competing viewpoints. Demand to see replication if it's a scientific claim. Stack up the supporting evidence that the claim is wrong.

Key Principles to Remember

1. The credibility of expertise should depend on:

- **Experience**
- ***Track record***
- **Intelligence**

Track record is **enormous**. If an expert has been consistently wrong in their predictions over time, why trust them now?

2. Watch for non-experts paraded as experts in the wrong field.

Just because someone is famous in one niche doesn't mean they know what they're talking about in another. A celebrity stockbroker might dominate the headlines, but that doesn't mean they understand macroeconomics better than someone with a background in data or economic theory.

In that example, we'd tend to think: *"Famous financial person = expert in all things finance."* But that's a trap.

Another example?

During the COVID pandemic, many medical doctors, skilled in clinical medicine, were outmaneuvered by statisticians and data analysts who understood population-level modeling. Expertise is not one-size-fits-all—context matters.

3. If a claim relies on a study, ask:

- Who paid for it?
- Who conducted it?
- Has it been reproduced?

Others cite numerous studies that are later debunked themselves. Some estimates suggest that up to 50% of peer-reviewed studies are later found to be invalid.[19,20,21]

---

19 Bolli, R. (2015). Reflections on the irreproducibility of scientific papers. *Circulation Research, 117*(8), 665–666. https://doi.org/10.1161/CIRCRESAHA.115.307496
20 Gwynne, P. (2016). Scientists face the cost of irreproducible results. *Research-Technology Management, 59*(3).
21 Benito, J. S., Alegre-Cebollada, J., Daura, X., & Giráldez, T. (2016). Irreproducibility in research: What can we do about it?

Trust but verify. Expertise is valuable—but not infallible. Always take claims, no matter how credentialed the source, **to court**.

Key Takeaways – Chapter 12: Appeal to Authority

- Appeal to authority accepts claims as accurate just because they come from someone with a title or status.
- Real expertise matters, but propaganda abuses the *appearance* of expertise to shut down debate.
- Credentials don't replace evidence—claims should still be questioned and tested.
- Gell-Mann Amnesia makes us forget how often "insiders" get it wrong ...but trust them again anyway.
- Always ask: Can this authority back up their claim with logic, evidence, and a proven track record?

You're doing great. Keep moving forward!

CHAPTER 13: Pinpointing the Enemy (Scapegoating)

This lesson explores the propaganda technique known as "pinpointing the enemy" or scapegoating. It illustrates how complex societal problems are often simplified to a single cause, group, or individual, creating a clear target for blame. This approach oversimplifies reality and enables manipulation through emotion, groupthink, and political agendas.

Definition: Pinpointing the enemy is a propaganda technique that reduces a complex problem to a single person, group, idea, or object, and suggests that the issue will be solved once that entity is eliminated or controlled.

Examples of Pinpointing the Enemy

Stalin's purge of the Kulaks is one of history's clearest examples. The Soviet regime took a complex economic and drought and hung it around the necks of one group: the Kulaks. These were relatively successful farmers who became the scapegoats for the nation's failures. The propaganda machine painted them as greedy hoarders sabotaging progress. What followed was horrifying—forced deportations, mass executions, and engineered famine.

Why did it work? Because humans crave simplicity. We hate uncertainty, and a clear villain helps us channel frustration. Propaganda takes advantage of this by giving people someone to blame—someone they can point to and say, "They're the problem."

It's also a powerful tool for unity. A shared enemy unites fractured groups.[22,23] Emotional satisfaction replaces confusion. And moral clarity—no matter how false—feels like purpose.

You still see it today. People blame one fast-food chain for the entire obesity epidemic. Politicians claim that if we just ban guns, murder will vanish. News anchors often point suggestive fingers at "the rich" for every economic problem, without context or nuance.

Psychology backs this up: shared enemies make people feel bonded, focused, and even energized. That's why propaganda rarely sticks to the facts—it sticks to a face. If it can't find a real villain, it creates one.

The claim relies on vilifying one party or object without acknowledging any other contributing factors.

Case Study: Pinpointing the Enemy

22 Hoyer, B., & De Jaegher, K. D. (2015). *Cooperation and the common enemy effect: A network disruption model.*
23 Salo, M., & Sinkko, R. (2012). *The science of unit cohesion: Its characteristics and impacts.*

Case Study NESTPAD:

Name the Emotion:

Fear, anger, relief, self-righteousness

Say the Technique:

Pinpointing the Enemy / Scapegoating

Prove the Claim:

Examine whether that person or group has truly caused the entire issue. Sometimes they have!!

And Disprove the Claim:

What are other possible causes of the strife?

Notice: When we are on the **D** of NESTPAD for this technique, list out alternative causes or contributing factors when scapegoating is identified. This helps avoid reductionist thinking and promotes balanced problem-solving.

Final Reminder: This technique is effective. Discuss it with the young people in your life, if age-appropriate. Teach them how dangerous scapegoating can be if you get this wrong as a problem-solving method.

Key Takeaways: Pinpointing the Enemy (Scapegoating)

- Scapegoating simplifies complex problems by blaming one person, group, or idea.
- It appeals to emotion, offering a false sense of clarity, unity, and moral righteousness.
- Propaganda uses it to manipulate public anger and redirect frustration toward easy targets.
- Psychology shows that shared enemies strengthen group bonds, even when the blame is misplaced.
- Counter it by identifying other contributing factors and resisting oversimplified narratives.

CHAPTER 14:
Cause and Effect Fallacy

Definition: Asserting a debatable cause-and-effect chain as fact.

This fallacy occurs when someone draws a direct causal link between two things without properly proving the connection, often because the two are merely correlated or the real cause lies elsewhere.

Examples:

- **Conversation:** "I took an aspirin, and my cold went away."
- **Advertisement:** "Our lavender oil will double your relaxation."
- **Politics:** "Carbon dioxide causes global temperature rise." (counterclaim: "Temperature rise causes carbon dioxide increase.")[24]

Notable Illustration: Al Gore's 2004 documentary *An Inconvenient Truth* used a famous scissor-lift scene to dramatize a claimed cause-effect relationship between CO_2 levels and global warming. In later years, some scientific analyses argued that temperature change may precede CO_2 increases in historical data, illustrating potential backward science.

Key Insight: This fallacy is a subtype of assertion. The message may be emotionally compelling and persuasive, but its logical foundation may be flawed.

24 Demetris Koutsoyiannis, "Stochastic Assessment of Temperature–CO_2 Causal Relationship in Climate from the Phanerozoic through Modern Times," *Mathematical Biosciences and Engineering 21*, no. 7 (2024): 6560–6602, https://doi.org/10.3934/mbe.2024287.

Case Study: Cause and Effect Fallacy

Case Study NESTPAD:

Name the Emotion:

Self-Satisfaction

Say the Technique:

Possible Cause – Effect Fallacy

Prove the Claim:

Examine the Study

And Disprove the Claim:

Find if there's a study that reverses cause and effect, or only finds correlation.

John T. Reed's Four Possibilities for Correlated Phenomena:

1. A causes B
2. B causes A
3. Coincidence/similarity
4. A and B caused by C (a third factor)

Your job when you spot this is to find out which of the above 4 is true.

Key Takeaways – Chapter 14: Cause and Effect Fallacy

- This fallacy assumes a direct cause-effect link without proving it, often confusing correlation with causation.
- It's persuasive because it simplifies complex issues into neat, emotional narratives.
- Real analysis requires testing if A causes B, B causes A, both are caused by C, or it's just coincidence.
- Headlines and ads frequently misuse this fallacy to sell ideas or products (or just to get you to click)
- Use NESTPAD and John T. Reed's four-part test to critically evaluate causal claims.

CHAPTER 15:
Ridicule

Definition:

Implying facts or logic are useless because the person, source, or idea doesn't deserve engagement.

Common Forms of Ridicule:

- **Name-calling / Ad Hominem:** Attacking the person instead of the argument (e.g., "Why listen to his advice on weightlifting? He's a pencil-neck.")
- **Genetic Fallacy:** Discrediting an idea based solely on its source (e.g., "That's from Fox News, so it must be wrong.")
- **Bulverism:** Assuming someone's argument is invalid solely because of their alleged motives or identity (e.g., "You only think that way because you're a woman.")

These techniques stop meaningful discussion by avoiding engagement with the actual ideas.

Case Study: Ridicule

Case Study NESTPAD:

Name the Emotion:

(Your initial emotion here would typically depend on whether the insulted woman is in your political 'tribe' or not.)

Say the Technique:

Appeal to Ridicule

Prove the Claim: (in this case, the insult draws us away from the issue... we must return to the claim)

Find the pros of the supported tax policy being discussed.

And Disprove the Claim:

Find the cons of the supported tax policy being discussed.

Why It Works:

- Ridicule taps into our emotional responses, like fear of social rejection or anger.
- The **Illusory Truth Effect** amplifies ridicule's impact—if we hear a slur or label repeated enough, we may start to believe it.

Final Note: This technique is rampant in media, politics, and daily life. Train yourself and your loved ones to recognize ridicule and dissect it with calm logic, rather than reacting with emotional acceptance.

Key Takeaways – Chapter 15: Ridicule

- Ridicule shuts down debate by mocking the person or source instead of addressing the argument.
- Common forms include name-calling, genetic fallacy, and Bulverism.
- It's emotionally compelling because it triggers social fear, anger, or tribal loyalty.
- Repeated ridicule can create false beliefs through the Illusory Truth Effect.
- Counter it by refocusing on the actual claim and analyzing both pros and cons logically.

We'll continue identifying manipulative rhetorical tools. Keep moving forward!

CHAPTER 16:
Transfer (False Connection)

Some of you are familiar with martial arts. In many disciplines, there's a strategy where you use your opponent's momentum against them. For instance, if someone charges at you, instead of resisting head-on, you might redirect their energy into a throw. Propaganda often uses a very similar tactic.

We all have tendencies—things we love, things we hate—and propagandists can manipulate those instincts. A nurturing mother can be exploited by a message disguised in maternal care. A testosterone-fueled young man can be manipulated through messages disguised as righteous aggression. That's the foundation of the propaganda technique called **transfer**.

Definition

Transfer (also known as false connection): Transferring feelings and associations from one idea, symbol, or person to another.

This is the propaganda equivalent of hiding a bitter pill in cheese. It pairs something people already like or trust (or loath or hate ... this can work both ways) with a new idea they want you to accept.

Examples

- **Conversation:** "Everyone who's a fascist is enlisting in the military."
  - Fascism and military service are being falsely linked.
- **Advertisement:** "Try Mentos. Einstein ate them."
  - Classic testimonial and transfer—associating genius with a mint.

- **Politics:** A candidate stands in front of an American flag to transfer feelings of patriotism to their candidacy.

More Examples

- "If you smoke Marlboros, you're a rugged cowboy."
- "If you support Trump, you're a Nazi."
- "If you support Obama, you're a communist."

Each one tries to shortcut reason by forcing associations into your subconscious.

Visual Examples

Case Study: Transfer

Case Study NESTPAD:

Name the Emotion:

Confidence in the message because of the lab coat

Say the Technique:

'This is transfer'

Prove the Claim:

What supporting evidence is there that I should take this pill 7 times a day?

And Disprove the Claim:

What are the downsides of taking this pill seven times a day?

Key Takeaways – Chapter 16: Transfer (False Connection)

- Transfer links questionably related ideas to manipulate emotions and shortcut critical thinking.
- It works by pairing something familiar or trusted with a new idea the propagandist wants you to accept.
- This technique is used in conversation, advertising, and politics to create false emotional associations.
- Always separate the symbol from the message and analyze the actual evidence behind the claim.

You're becoming more con proof with every chapter. Keep moving forward!

CHAPTER 17:
Ignoring Net Effect

I have a lot of respect for both of my grandfathers. One of them spent his entire career working for Ralston Purina—the company behind Dog Chow. In the third grade, my teacher told us that world hunger could be solved if we just redirected all the money spent on dog food to help the poor. I repeated this at a family dinner later that week, and my practical-minded grandfather didn't miss a beat. He fired off questions: "Would you get rid of all the dogs?" "Who decides how the money gets distributed?" "So... dog owners are responsible for world hunger, but non-pet owners aren't? Walk me through that." He was a kind man, but he had no patience for sloppy thinking, and that moment taught me a lasting lesson: bold claims without weighing the trade-offs are just noise.

That's what this lesson is all about: **ignoring the net effect**, one of the most common propaganda techniques.

Definition

Ignoring the net effect means mentioning either the benefits without the costs or the costs without the benefits. If a message only gives you one side of the coin, you're not getting the truth—you're getting propaganda.

Examples

- **Conversation:** "The government should give everyone $10,000 a month. We'd all be better off!"

- **Advertising:** (ALL ads to this—highlighting benefits while ignoring downsides, costs, or limitations.)
- **Politics:** "Our new jobs program will create millions of jobs!" (But fails to mention those jobs have worker-group-A breaking windows, and worker-group-B replacing them—see: the Broken Window Fallacy.)

Economists often capture this concept of 'net effect' with the phrase: **"There are no solutions, only trade-offs."**

The McNamara Fallacy

The McNamara fallacy is related to our 'ignoring net effect' issue. It's when you track the easy-to-measure metrics and ignore the harder, more meaningful ones.

Example: A traffic czar introduces a 5-mph speed limit to reduce fatalities by 95%. Yes, the deaths may drop, but what happens to commerce, productivity, and supply chains? Trade-offs matter.

Case Study: Ignoring Net Effect

Exactly right. No one wants car crashes—but if we don't weigh the cost of the solution, we're not thinking clearly.

Case Study NESTPAD:

Name the Emotion:

Relief! (There's someone who can fix the problem of traffic fatalities!)

Say the Technique:

'This is ignoring the net effect.'

(THERE IS NO 'PAD' HERE)

When you spot 'ignoring net effect', list out the costs of reducing the speed limit to 5 mph vs the cost of not doing it.

'Ignoring Net Effect' is especially common when:

- The topic is very complex.
- There's an emotional appeal.
- Think tanks or experts push a specific agenda.

Pro Tip: When an expert unveils a "bold new idea," follow the money. Who's funding their institution? Is there a long chain of NGOs obscuring the source? That paper trail often reveals the true agenda. Many think tanks aren't neutral at all—they're polished PR machines, repackaging corporate or political interests in the language of expertise.

Key Insight: The more complex the issue, the more likely it is that someone will leave out critical details. Don't fall for "half-pinions" — opinions that criticize without offering real alternatives. If someone says, "Country A shouldn't retaliate," ask, "Then what should they do?" Partial answers are not enough. Always demand the whole picture.

Key Takeaways – Chapter 17: Ignoring Net Effect

- This technique highlights benefits or costs while deliberately ignoring the trade-offs.
- Propaganda thrives on one-sided messaging. Truth requires the whole picture.
- Complex issues often hide costs behind emotional appeals or bold claims.
- The McNamara Fallacy focuses only on measurable metrics, ignoring real-world consequences.
- Always ask: What are the hidden costs or downsides? Every solution has trade-offs.

Your brain is getting bigger. Keep moving forward!

CHAPTER 18:
Appeal to Victimhood

Do you remember a few lessons ago when I talked about transfer and compared it to martial arts—how you use your opponent's momentum to take them down? Well, appeal to pity is another propaganda technique that works similarly. If you have a big heart, this one's going to hit home.

Definition: Appeal to victimhood (also called appeal to pity) is when someone distracts from the relevant points of a topic by using pity. It's weaponized compassion. Instead of focusing on the logic or facts, the emotional weight of suffering is used to steer your opinion.

Examples:

- **Conversation:** "The teacher should give Rick an A. He studied all night even though his grandmother just died."
- **Politics:** "We need to give $1 trillion to starving puppies in Bangladesh."
  This example is intentionally exaggerated, but notice how the emotional trigger is used to bypass scrutiny. If you object, you risk being perceived as heartless.
- **Media:** President Jones recommits to his promise that every sick infant will receive free healthcare from the federal government.
  - What does this do to someone trying to raise fiscal concerns? It makes them appear monstrous.

Important Insight: In our current culture, emotional blackmail is everywhere. Leaders and activists compete for underdog status because it grants the moral high ground. This isn't inherently evil, but it becomes propaganda when it distracts from cost, complexity, or counterarguments.

This chapter is not saying, "don't help sick babies." It's saying: if an argument or policy can't stand up under scrutiny without emotional pressure, that's a red flag.

CASE STUDY APPEAL TO VICTIMHOOD

NEST PAD:

- **Name the Emotion:** Sadness. Compassion. A sense of obligation.
- **Say the Technique:** Appeal to victimhood (or appeal to pity).
- **Prove the Claim:** Would the proposed action (e.g., national sick-infant policy) actually solve the problem as promised?
- **And Disprove the Claim:** What are the trade-offs? Could it be logistically or economically unfeasible? Is there a better way to help?

This one takes maturity to confront. But if you can recognize it, especially when the messaging pulls your heartstrings, you'll be much harder to manipulate.

Key Takeaways :

- Appeal to victimhood uses emotional suffering to distract from facts and logic.
- It manipulates compassion to shut down debate and gain the moral high ground.
- This technique often makes counterarguments seem heartless, regardless of merit.
- It's not wrong to care, but outcomes (not just intentions) must inform decision-making.
- Stay grounded: if an idea collapses without emotional pressure, it needs more scrutiny.

Your brain is growing up. You're getting harder to manipulate! Keep moving forward.

CHAPTER 19:
Card Stacking

Definition

Card stacking is a propaganda technique that involves misrepresenting information by minimizing or omitting opposing data or viewpoints, thereby creating an unbalanced picture. The "stacked deck" may seem complete, but you're only seeing the cards they want you to see.

This technique can appear in:

- Biased documentaries
- Skewed search engine results
- Unbalanced answers in an AI Bot
- Algorithm-fed social media feeds
- Interviews or panels where the "opposition" is token or weakened

Examples

- **Conversation:**

  "Did you see that documentary on how bad nuclear energy is? It only had one 15-second clip from someone saying it was safe."

This is a classic case of card stacking—a one-sided presentation while technically allowing a "token" dissenting voice.

▶ **Recruitment:**

EMBARK ON THE JOURNEY OF A LIFETIME

Minimum 2-year enlistment required (see fine print and color blended letters)

▶ **Visual Media:**

Before-and-after fitness photos often feature poor lighting, slouched posture, an unpleasant frown, or oversized clothes in the "before" photo; it's visual card stacking.

▶ **Censorship:**

When the opposing view is suppressed entirely—algorithmically or manually—that's an extreme and dangerous form of card stacking.

Quick Tip for Parents & Kids

"If it sounds too good to be true, it probably is."

Your mom's advice wasn't just wise—it was *anti-propaganda training. If she was teaching you this, she was giving you the informal card stacking lecture. As a child, the downsides are minimized or hidden from you often in marketing.*

Case Study Example

How to Develop Immunity: NEST PAD

- **Name the Emotion:**
  "This documentary convinced me that everything bad I've heard about Michael Jackson was false.

- **Say the Technique:**
  "I've been cardstacked. I only heard claims that supported one side of the issue.

- **Prove the Claim:**
  Seek out credible sources that support the claims in the documentary you just watched

- **And Disprove the Claim:**
  Seek out credible counterpoints or evidence from opposing perspectives in documentaries that have concluded that the Michael Jackson allegations appear valid.

Final Insight

Just because you've watched a two-hour podcast featuring one expert or read a 40-page think tank white paper doesn't mean you're fully informed. If you've only seen one side, your "courtroom" is missing a defense attorney. Don't make decisions based only on the prosecution's case.

Key Takeaways – Chapter 19: Card Stacking

- Card stacking hides or downplays opposing views to create a biased, one-sided narrative.
- It appears in media, ads, search results, and social platforms through selective presentation or censorship.
- Even minimal opposition—like a token voice—doesn't balance a stacked message.
- Visual tactics (e.g., lighting, framing) can also skew perception in "before and after" comparisons.
- Always ask: What's missing from this picture? Seek out both sides before forming conclusions.

The card-stacking lesson will keep you from getting duped. You're doing great. Keep moving forward!

CHAPTER 20:
Composition and Division Fallacies

Introduction

Our brains crave shortcuts—and that includes making quick judgments based on limited information. PR machines and spin-masters take advantage of this. Two of the most common shortcuts in propaganda are the fallacies of composition and division. These are mental traps that confuse parts with wholes, and vice versa.

Definition

- **Composition Fallacy:** Assuming what's true of the part must be true of the whole.
  → *Judging the symphony by a single note.*
- **Division Fallacy:** Assuming what's true of the whole must be true of each part.
  → *Judging a note based on the whole symphony.*

Examples

Composition Fallacy

- "Timmy got arrested. He goes to that school, so the whole school must be full of criminals."
- "A Republican bombed a clinic. Republicans are terrorists."

Division Fallacy

- "That sorority is full of snobs. Sally is in it, so she must be one too."

- "Libertarians avoid war. Bob is a libertarian. Bob must be soft on crime."

Why This Matters

- **Composition fallacies** are often used to smear large groups—religious, political, or ethnic.
- **Division fallacies** lead to stereotyping individuals based on their affiliations.
- Propaganda thrives on these shortcuts: marketers, insurance companies, and governments all use statistical profiling. But individualizing people based solely on group traits? That's lazy—and dangerous.

Case Study – *Card Stacking*

How to Build Immunity: NEST PAD

- **Name the Emotion:** "I feel disgusted by corruption in that party."
- **Say the Technique:** "That's a composition fallacy."
- **Prove the Claim:** "Is there evidence the entire system causes that behavior?"

- **And Disprove the Claim:** "Can I find counterexamples that break the pattern?"
- **Always ask:** Is this person typical, or an outlier?

Final Word

We live in a society that both relies on stereotyping and condemns it. Some industries, such as insurance or marketing, use group data out of necessity. It's not wrong to recognize patterns when the math supports it (for example, young men statistically take more risks on the road). What is bad is using that data to judge an individual unfairly. The key is this: analyze the group but treat the person in front of you as unique.

Key Takeaways

- Don't judge a group by one member (composition fallacy), or a person by the group they're in (division fallacy).
- Sometimes it's appropriate to judge a group by its mission and an individual by their actions—wisdom is knowing when to do what.
- These fallacies are emotional shortcuts that feed stereotyping and manipulation.
- Use NEST PAD to slow down and challenge the assumption.
- Your ability to think depends on distinguishing between patterns that matter and generalizations that don't.

CHAPTER 21:
Loaded and Vague Words

Definition

Loaded and vague words are terms that carry powerful emotional associations or multiple meanings, depending on who's using or hearing them.

They bypass the rational mind and go straight to the emotions.

Why It Matters

Loaded terms are a favorite weapon of propagandists because they hijack your emotional reactions and stop critical thought.

They are commonly found in:

- News headlines
- Political speeches
- Activist slogans
- Social media arguments

They also show up in loaded questions, which are questions that contain a hidden assertion, forcing you to accept a premise just by answering.

Examples of Loaded Words in Use

- **In Conversation**
  "I saw your Instagram post of the shock collar—do you still abuse your dog?"

- **In Politics**
  "Don't vote for Bill. He wore a leprechaun costume on St. Patrick's Day. He's clearly racist toward the Irish."

CASE STUDY: LOADED TERMS

Count how many emotionally loaded terms are in that sentence. (Hint: it's a lot.)

Loaded Questions – What Are They?

A **loaded question** includes an embedded assumption.

"Do you still beat your wife?"
If you answer yes or no, you're still accepting the frame of guilt.

How to Respond in Conversation

If someone uses a **loaded term** or **question** in a live discussion:

- Pause the conversation.
- Say: "We need to define our terms before we go further."
- If it's a loaded question: "Sorry, I have a rule—I don't answer loaded questions. Happy to clarify if we define the premise."

If it's in writing (a headline, post, etc.), don't accept the emotional bait. Step back and analyze.

Developing Immunity: NESTPAD

Name the Emotion

> *"That made me feel angry and disgusted."*

Say the Technique

> *"That's a loaded term being used to bypass my logic."*

Prove the Claim

Look for objective definitions and facts. Is this term ever defined clearly? What actions or evidence support it?

And

Disprove the Claim

Look for opposing interpretations, alternate definitions, or evidence that the label is misleading or misapplied.

COMMON LOADED TERMS AT THE TIME OF THIS WRITING

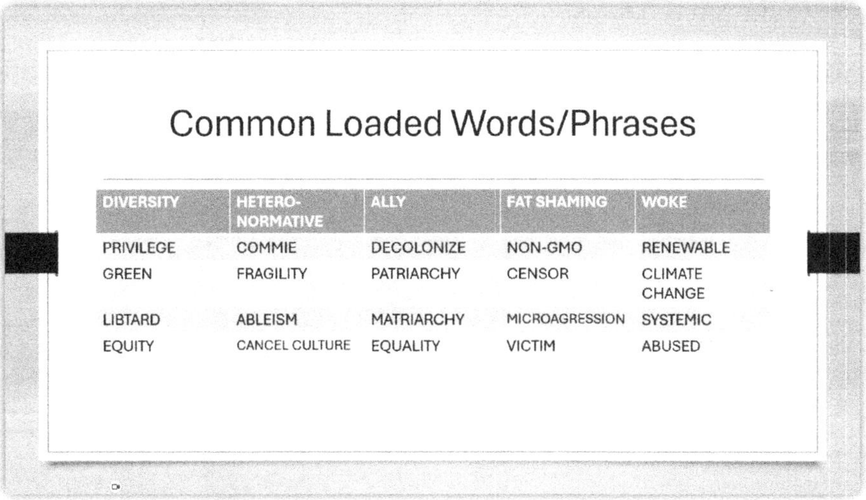

Common Loaded Words/Phrases

DIVERSITY	HETERO-NORMATIVE	ALLY	FAT SHAMING	WOKE
PRIVILEGE	COMMIE	DECOLONIZE	NON-GMO	RENEWABLE
GREEN	FRAGILITY	PATRIARCHY	CENSOR	CLIMATE CHANGE
LIBTARD	ABLEISM	MATRIARCHY	MICROAGRESSION	SYSTEMIC
EQUITY	CANCEL CULTURE	EQUALITY	VICTIM	ABUSED

Key Reminders

- You **cannot have an honest conversation** when loaded language is the starting point.
- Loaded terms are **not neutral**. If someone won't define them, that's a red flag.
- **The illusory truth effect** says that if you hear a loaded word or an idea often enough, you will believe it. Don't let repetition trick you.

Pro Tip: If necessary, stop mid-conversation and ask, "What do you mean by that word?" If the other person resists defining it, they're probably relying on propaganda.

Key Takeaways – Chapter 21: Loaded and Vague Words

- Loaded and vague words are designed to trigger emotion and shut down critical thinking.
- They're common in headlines, political talk, social media, and activist language.
- Loaded questions trap you into accepting false assumptions just by answering.
- Always pause and ask for clear definitions—vague or undefined terms are red flags.

You'll start seeing loaded terms everywhere now. Stay sharp. Keep moving forward!

CHAPTER 22: Contextomies

Definition

A **contextomy** is the **manipulation of meaning by removing key context.**

It makes someone **look guilty, racist, violent, or heroic,** depending on what parts are **edited out**.

Why It Matters

- This technique is **lethal to truth**.
- It relies entirely on **missing information** to **change a person's memory or belief.**
- It's often behind **viral lies**, **political slander**, and even the **Mandela Effect**—that eerie sensation of remembering something "wrong."

Examples

Conversation

> *"No, no, I saw it with my own eyes.*
> *He was hitting him for no reason."*

(But they didn't see what happened 10 seconds earlier.)

Politics

> *"I can't believe Elizabeth Warren gave a Nazi salute!"*
> *(She was waving, and they froze the frame.)*

Media

> *"Trump called neo-Nazis 'very fine people.'"*
> *(What was edited out: "I'm not talking about neo-Nazis and white nationalists, because they should be condemned totally.")*

Why It Works

- Our brains **believe what we see** and **trust repetition.**
- Contextomies exploit **low-information environments.**
- They're hard to refute because:
- They use authentic **images or video,**
- They exploit our **confirmation bias,**
- They often align with pre-existing beliefs.

CASE STUDIES

Elizabeth Warren Nazi Salute Hoax

In 2016, a Twitter user accused Elizabeth Warren of performing a Nazi salute by using a still image. She was in the middle of waving to the crowd, and yet this still image leaves no context for the motion of her hand. This mischaracterized the meaning of her hand in the air completely.

Trump's "Very Fine People" Hoax

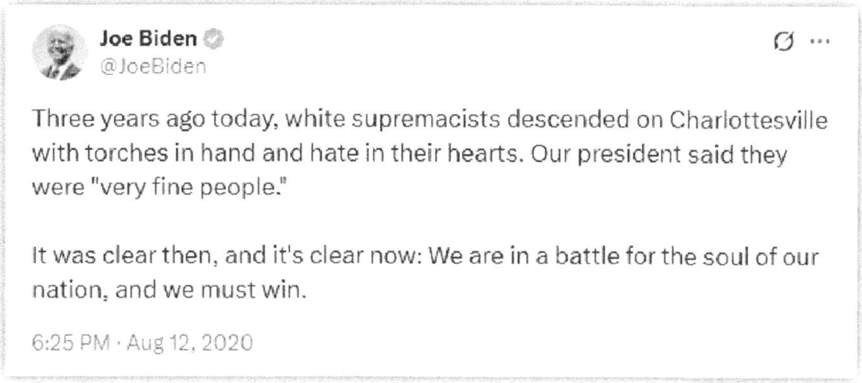

Joe Biden
@JoeBiden

Three years ago today, white supremacists descended on Charlottesville with torches in hand and hate in their hearts. Our president said they were "very fine people."

It was clear then, and it's clear now: We are in a battle for the soul of our nation, and we must win.

6:25 PM · Aug 12, 2020

Here is the whole transcript of Trump's original comment:

Reporter: The Neo-Nazis started this thing. They showed up in Charlottesville.

Trump: Excuse me, they didn't put themselves down as Neo-Nazis, and you had some very bad people in that group. ***But you also had people that were very fine people, on both sides.*** *You had people in that group — excuse me, excuse me, I saw the same pictures as you did — you had people in that group that were there to protest the taking down of, to them, a very very important statue and the renaming of a park from Robert E. Lee to another name. George Washington was a slave owner. Was George Washington a slave owner? So will George Washington now lose his status, are we gonna take down — excuse me — are we gonna take down statues of George Washington? How about Thomas Jefferson? What do you think of Thomas Jefferson? You like him? Okay good. Are we gonna take down the statue? Cause he was a major slaveowner. Now are we gonna take down his statue? So you know what? It's fine. You're changing history, you're changing culture, and you had people —* ***and I'm not talking about the Neo-Nazis and the white nationalists, because they should be condemned totally****. But you had many people in that group other than Neo-Nazis and white nationalists, okay? And the press has treated them absolutely unfairly. Now, in the other group also, you had some fine people, but you also had troublemakers, and you see them come with the black out-*

fits, and with the helmets, and the baseball bats, you got a lot of bad people in the other group too.[25]

How to Defend Against It

- If it sounds **crazy**, **evil**, or **too perfect**, assume you're missing something.
- **Don't trust headlines** or viral images without investigating the surrounding footage or full transcript.

Tools That Help

- **GroundNews.com** – Tracks political bias across media stories.
- **Community Notes on X** /X – Fact-checks viral posts through crowdsourced context and notes.

NEST PAD – Contextomy Immunity

Name the Emotion

"This story made me furious! I feel disgusted."

Say the Technique

"This might be a contextomy—this story is too crazy to be true, but I might not be seeing the full picture."

Prove the Claim

"Is there full footage? A transcript? Can I find the original statement?"

And Disprove the Claim

"Does this contradict other known facts? Did the speaker clarify elsewhere? Was this edited?"

25 Vox Staff, "Full Transcript: Trump's Press Conference Defending His Charlottesville Remarks," *Vox*, August 15, 2017, https://www.vox.com/2017/8/15/16154028/trump-press-conference-transcript-charlottesville.

Final Thoughts

Contextomies are **weapons-grade propaganda**.

They're especially dangerous because they **can't be combated with logic alone**—you must **recover the missing pieces**.

If you ever feel **sure** about something that seems extreme, ask:

"What am I not seeing?"

That question might save your mind.

Key Takeaways – Chapter 22: Contextomies

- A **contextomy** distorts meaning by cutting out key context, twisting reality to smear or praise someone unfairly.
- It often underlies viral lies, political slander, and false memories (e.g., the *Mandela Effect*).
- This tactic works because it uses real footage or images, exploits confirmation bias, and plays into what people already believe.
- Headlines, frozen frames, and clipped quotes are red flags—**always seek the whole video or transcript.**
- Use NEST PAD to slow down, question the emotion, and ask: *"What am I not seeing?"*

Congratulations! You've covered the most popular and fundamental techniques of the modern era!

Next, we'll move on to discover the most common way we're manipulated with numbers...

SECTION III - THE NUMBERS CAN LIE

Overview

This chapter marks the beginning of a new section focused on how statistics, graphs, and percentages can be used deceptively, especially in media, courtrooms, and public policy. While many people instinctively trust numbers, data can be misused to create propaganda just as easily as words.

Example: Sally Clark (True Story)

- **Tragic story from the UK**
  Sally Clark was a mother whose two babies died from **SIDS (sudden infant death syndrome)** several years apart.
- **Expert misuse of statistics**
  A respected pediatrician testified that the odds of two SIDS deaths in the same family were **1 in 73 million**. This figure came from **squaring** the odds of one SIDS death (1 in 8,543).
- **Fatal error**
  The assumption was that the two deaths were **independent events**, but **they weren't**. Medical evidence suggesting a common cause was excluded.

- **Result**
  Clark was wrongly convicted of murder, spent **3 years in prison**, and eventually **took her own life**.

Lesson: Even *solid math* can be misused when key assumptions are mistaken or hidden

Example 2: "The Murder Rate Has Doubled in Singapore!"

- Sounds terrifying... until you learn:
  - Last year: 1 murder
  - This year: 2 murders
- The rate *did* double. But going from 1 to 2 murders in a city of 6 million is **statistically insignificant**.

Lesson: A percentage without **raw numbers** (or raw numbers without a percentage) is likely propaganda.

Example 3: "A New Virus Has a 50% Fatality Rate"

WHAT'S SELDOM (IF EVER) EXPLAINED BY THE NEWS

THERE ARE TWO FATALITY RATES

- Reported fatality rate = **CFR** (Case Fatality Rate):
  = deaths ÷ confirmed cases
- But the more accurate measure = **IFR** (Infection Fatality Rate):
  = deaths ÷ total infected
- At the beginning of an outbreak, **many infections are uncounted**, making CFR **wildly inflated**.

Lesson: Early pandemic numbers are often **misleading by design**—high fear = high engagement.

NEST PAD – Dealing with Deceptive Numbers

Name the **E**motion

> *"This stat makes me terrified!"*

Say the **T**echnique

> *"They're using* **statistical manipulation** *or* **missing context**.*"*

Prove It

> *"Let's check the source. Does it include all infections?"*

And

Disprove It

> *"Are there alternative interpretations? Was another factor ignored?"*

Final Thoughts

You're now stepping into the world of **numerical propaganda**. This intro showed how **even accurate math** can be **weaponized by omission, false assumptions, or mislabeling.** By the end of this module, you'll be better prepared to see through the statistical smoke and mirrors that dominate public debate.

Next lesson: Common ways statistics are warped. Stay sharp.

CHAPTER 23:
Built-In Sample Bias

Let's start with a simple question:

Could I run a poll that says 90% of Americans hate chocolate? Or that 99% of the population despises dogs?

It sounds ridiculous. But if I knew how to manipulate the **sample**, I could pull it off. That's the scary part. Numbers don't need to be forged—they need to be **framed**. This chapter is about how people rig the **starting line** of data collection to steer you toward a false conclusion before the math even starts. The weapon? **Built-in sample bias.**

What Is a Sample, and Why Does It Matter?

You can't survey 8 billion people. So, we use samples—a small slice of the population meant to represent the whole. The keyword is "represent." Good researchers work diligently to ensure the accuracy of their samples. Bad actors, on the other hand, don't want the truth. They want persuasion disguised as data.

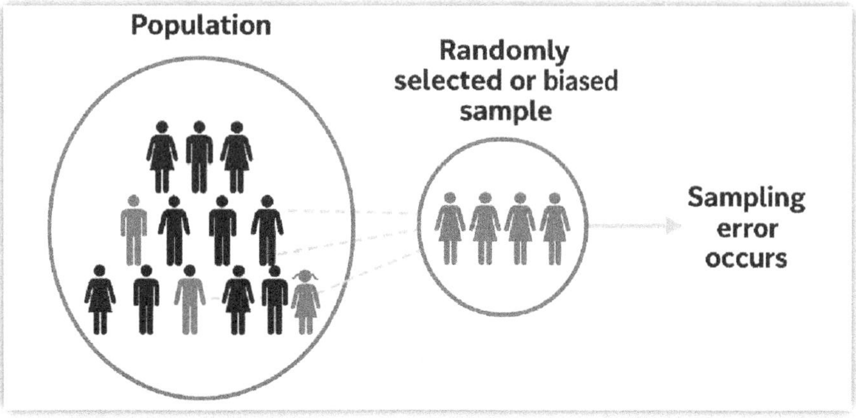

How Sample Bias Happens

Let's say the alumni magazine of Totally Elite University (TEU) reports that the average graduate makes $300,000 a year. Impressive, right? Until you learn how they got that number.

- TEU has 100,000 graduates from the past 50 years.
- The survey was based on 300 responses.

Now here's the problem:

- **Low earners** might skip the survey out of embarrassment (non-response bias).
- **High earners** might exaggerate their income to impress (self-inflation).
- **Affluent alumni** are more likely to stay connected and reachable (access bias).

Add it all up, and you get a shiny statistic that doesn't reflect reality. That's built-in sample bias: the data was warped **before** the first average was even calculated.

Common Ways Sampling Gets Rigged

Let's look at a few classic tactics used—intentionally or not—to bias a sample:

- **Selection Bias:** The way you choose your sample doesn't match the population. For example, only polling social media users skews younger and more online.

- **Non-response Bias:** People who don't respond may differ significantly from those who do.
- **Coverage Bias:** Some types of people are left out of the sample entirely, like polling only registered voters and ignoring the rest.
- **Sampling Error:** The sample size is too small or too specific to draw valid conclusions.
- **Question Framing Bias:** The way a question is worded nudges the respondent in a direction.
- **Interviewer Bias:** The tone, body language, or phrasing used by the person asking questions can influence the answers.
- **Social Desirability Bias:** People give answers they think are socially acceptable, not necessarily truthful.

Case Study: The Literary Digest Poll (1936)

In 1936, the magazine *Literary Digest* conducted a massive poll to predict the outcome of the U.S. presidential election. They surveyed millions—sounds impressive, right?

The problem is that their sample came from telephone **directories and car registrations**. In the middle of the Great Depression, this overrepresented wealthier Americans (those most likely to oppose FDR).

Result? The poll predicted a landslide win for Alf Landon. Reality? Roosevelt won in a landslide.

The size of the sample didn't matter. The bias was built in from the start.

How to Spot a Biased Sample

To protect yourself from fake numbers wrapped in statistical language, ask these questions:

1. **Was the sample representative?** Did everyone in the population have a fair shot at being included?
2. **Who paid for the study?** Follow the money.
3. **Has it been replicated?** Real findings can be repeated.
4. **What's the source's track record?** Do they have a history of accuracy or agenda-driven noise?

5. **What methodology was used?** Was it a random sample? Convenience sample? Online-only? Were the questions asked in person, on the phone, or via email?

The method matters as much as the math.

Your Shield Against Biased Samples

Here's your checklist for building immunity:

- Ask: "Did every individual have an equal chance of being selected?"
- Investigate the source and who funded it.
- Dig deeper into how the data was collected—sampling method, survey design, and even how the question was phrased.
- Look for red flags like small sample sizes, vague descriptions, or conclusions that happen to align perfectly with the sponsor's agenda.

Sampling bias is sneaky. It doesn't tamper with the math—it tampers with the **input**. But once you learn to spot it, you'll see through a lot of polished lies passed off as science.

Key Takeaways – Chapter 23: Built-In Sample Bias

- **Sample bias manipulates data before the math even begins**, by rigging who gets asked or how questions are framed.
- Even credible-looking stats can be fake if the sample is skewed, too small, or unrepresentative.
- Common tactics include **selection bias, non-response bias, coverage gaps, and loaded questions.**
- A large sample doesn't guarantee truth—h**ow the sample is selected matters more than size.**
- Always ask: *Who was surveyed, who paid for it, and does the sample truly represent the whole population?*

Let's keep building the shield. The next chapter arms you for another data deception.

CHAPTER 24:
The Well-Chosen Average

If you've got an agenda, being vague can sometimes be your best friend, especially when it comes to numbers. That's precisely what we're looking at in this lesson: how averages can be weaponized to mislead people without technically lying.

This is one of the easiest propaganda techniques to understand. It's also one of the most common.

The Trick with "Average"

Averages sound trustworthy. They give people a false sense of mathematical precision. But not all averages are created equal. When someone says, "The average person does X," what do they mean? Are they talking about the **mean**, the **median**, or the **mode**?

Let's look at a clear-cut example.

Suppose you run a small newsletter with 10 subscribers. You're trying to sell ad space to a luxury brand, so you make a bold claim: "Our average subscriber is a multimillionaire."

Sounds impressive, right?

Well, here's the truth. Nine of your ten subscribers are regular folks. One of them is worth $230 billion. Technically, if you take the **mean**—you add up everyone's net worth and divide by 10—you do get an "average" subscriber who's worth $22 billion.

But that's nonsense. You're using a single outlier to distort the whole picture.

Mean, Median, and Mode: A Quick Review

- **Mean:** This is the standard "average"—add all the values, divide by the number of values.
- **Median:** The middle value in a sorted list. Half the values fall above it, half fall below.
- **Mode:** The number that appears most often in a dataset.

Using our newsletter example:

- The **mean** is $22 billion.
- The **median** (the actual midpoint) might be something like $131,000.
- The **mode**—the most common net worth—could be $75,000.

Only one of these paints an honest picture. And it's not the mean.

Why It Matters

This kind of trickery shows up everywhere: in advertisements, political arguments, press releases, and especially scientific reports aimed at a general audience. If someone wants to sell you a narrative, they'll pick the version of "average" that helps their case the most.

It's subtle, but powerful. That's why it's crucial to ask: what kind of average are we talking about?

How to Defend Against It

Like always, we use the NESTPAD process.

- **Name the emotion** the number triggered. Maybe you felt impressed, or perhaps it triggered envy or fear.
- **Say the technique**: 'This could be a 'well-chosen average'... What am I looking at?
  (Once you confirm what it is, you can ...)
- **Prove** the claim.
- **And**
- **Disprove** the claim.

If you can't determine what kind of average is being used, be skeptical. In agenda-driven messaging, vagueness is not a bug—it's the point.

Key Takeaways – Chapter 24: The Well-Chosen Average

- Not all "averages" are the same—**mean, median, and mode** can tell radically different stories.
- Propagandists often pick the **most flattering or shocking average** to manipulate perception without technically lying.
- Outliers can **distort the mean**, making a situation seem richer, poorer, better, or worse than it is.
- Always ask: *Which kind of average is being used, and would a different one change the picture?*
- Use NESTPAD to pause, question the number, and test whether it's **a tool of truth or a trick of presentation**.

Let's move on to the next lesson.

CHAPTER 29:

The Small Sample Con

One of the most effective ways to manipulate data, by far, is to use a sample size that's too small. The trick works because people often assume that any number backed by data must be trustworthy. But if the sample is tiny, the conclusions are meaningless at best—and dishonest at worst.

How It Works

The small sample con is simple: a company or individual runs a "scientific study" or "trial" using a tiny group, just large enough to obtain the desired results. Then they parade the result around as if it's some groundbreaking, statistically sound finding.

Let's say a supplement company wants to claim, "Our mushroom powder improves mental focus in 75% of users."

That sounds compelling, right?

Here's how they might do it:

- They pick a group of just 12 users.
- They ask each one to rate their mental focus before and after using the product.
- If the first group doesn't deliver the desired results, they throw out the data and start over.
- Eventually, they get a group where 9 out of 12 report improvement—and now they have their 75%.

Is the claim technically true? Sure. Is it meaningful? Not even close.

Why It Works

It works because of the law of small numbers. In small samples, randomness can create big swings. Flip a coin 12 times and you might get 9 heads. Flip it a million times and you'll land closer to a 50/50 split.

That's why casinos love roulette streaks. You'll see five reds in a row and think black is "due." But it's all noise. Without a large enough dataset, patterns don't mean much.

A Real-World Example

In his classic book *How to Lie with Statistics*, Darrell Huff tells the story of a small polio vaccine trial. In this case[26].

- 450 children received the vaccine.
- 680 children did not (they were the control group).
- After an outbreak, none of the vaccinated kids got polio.

That sounds like a huge success—until you look deeper.

None of the control group kids got polio either. That's because the paralysis rate for polio in that outbreak was just 0.2%. Statistically, the study was too small to prove anything.

They later calculated that they would have needed approximately 17,000 participants to detect any meaningful difference.

What Makes a Study "Significant"

In statistics, the threshold for significance is typically defined by a value called alpha, commonly set at 5%. That means there's only a 5% chance the result happened by random luck.

- If your study has a **10%** alpha, it's shaky.
- If you reach **1%,** that's strong evidence that your result is real.
- But no matter what, if your sample size is too small, significance becomes nearly impossible to achieve—unless you rig the game.

26 Darrell Huff, *How to Lie with Statistics*, reissue ed. (New York: W. W. Norton & Company, 1993).

How to Defend Against It

If someone makes a bold claim based on a "study," ask:

- How many people were in the study?
- Who paid for it?
- Was it reproduced?
- Was the sample large enough for statistical significance?

If the sample is tiny, toss the claim.

The small sample con is just another form of cherry-picking, dressed up in a lab coat. Please don't fall for it. Teach your loved ones not to either.

Key Takeaways – Chapter 29: The Small Sample Con

- **Small sample sizes** can create misleading results that look scientific but are statistically worthless.
- Manipulators often rerun trials until they get the outcome they want, then present it as solid evidence.
- The **law of small numbers** means randomness creates fake patterns in tiny groups, but people fall for them.
- Always ask: *How big was the sample? Was it repeated? Who funded it?* If it's small, **the result is likely noise.**
- Teach your kids: **science needs scale—**real conclusions require large, unbiased, and repeatable studies.

You are getting manipulation proof! You're doing great. Keep moving forward.

CHAPTER 30: Misleading Graphs

One of the most powerful ways to manipulate you with numbers is not through the numbers themselves, but through how they're pictured. A graph can leave a stronger impression than a spreadsheet ever could. And that's the problem: the emotional impact of an image can override your ability to think clearly. Let's look at how this works.

The Graph Trick

Don't underestimate the power of a glance. One politician claims treasury revenue is soaring. His opponent says it's barely moved—and that's why you should vote for him. Most voters tune out when they hear numbers. But our brains are wired to respond to images. So, the first politician shows the graph on the left. The second shows the one on the right. Here's the wild part: both graphs are telling the truth. They're using the same data.

The Gee-Whiz Graph

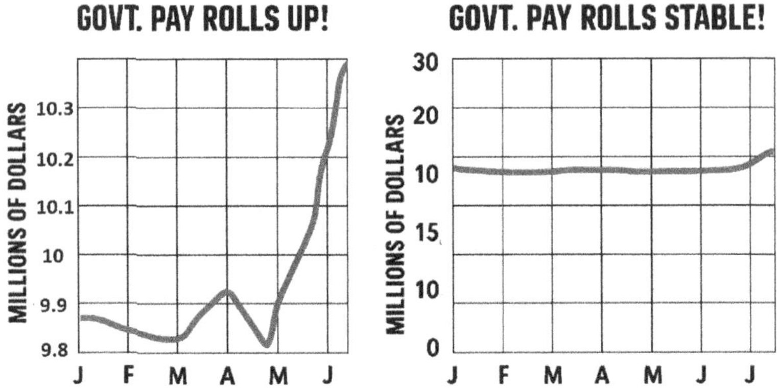

Watch the Axis Lines

Notice the trick? On the left, the y-axis starts around 9.8 million. That exaggerates tiny changes and makes the line shoot upward like a rocket. On the right, the y-axis begins at zero. Suddenly, that same growth looks flat and dull. The same data shows a different picture.

Whenever a graph's y-axis doesn't start at zero, be suspicious. It's often a visual stunt to warp your perception. Always check the scale.

Real World Examples

Quick reminder: Whenever I use real-world examples (like the next few), I'm not taking sides. I'm not advocating for or against the issue in the example. For the sake of these lessons, I'm politically neutral. The goal is to help you recognize deception or misrepresentation, no matter who's doing it or which "team" it's coming from. On we go....

The Zoom Trick

Another manipulation involves zooming in on a short timeframe, which often distorts the Y-axis of a graph. During the COVID pandemic, media outlets sometimes presented daily case graphs showing alarming spikes. At first glance, it looked like infections were going to doom everyone.

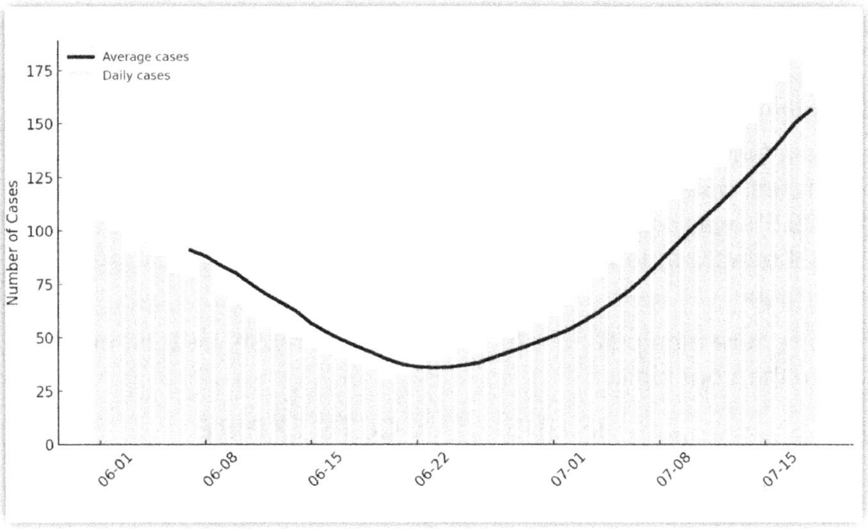

Media images like this were common during the COVID years. Let's see what the data representation looks like when we zoom out quite a bit...

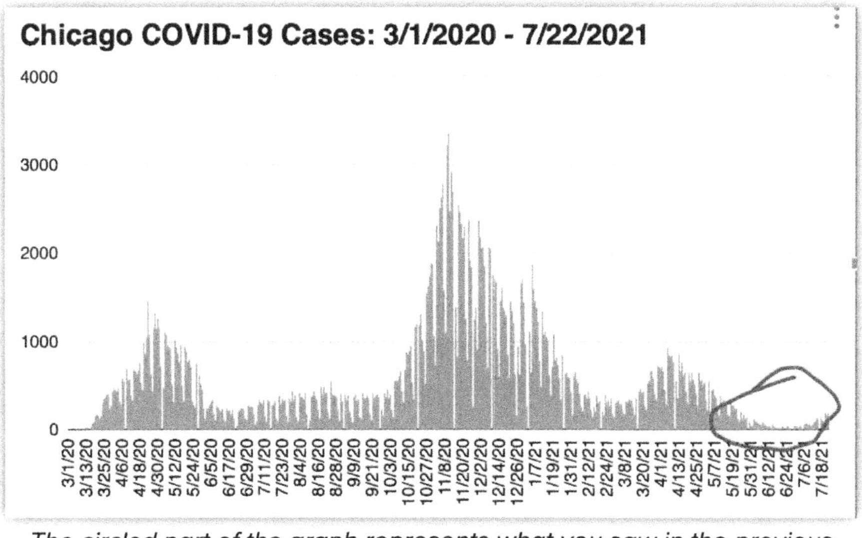

The circled part of the graph represents what you saw in the previous graph. It feels different. Yes?

Always ask: *What's missing? What's outside this frame?*

Bar Graph Shenanigans

Sometimes visual distortion doesn't even require fancy tricks—just a bad-faith design.

Take a famous example from cable news. A bar chart compares two tax rates: 35% vs. 39.6%. The actual difference is 4.6%. But the bar for 39.6% was drawn about five times taller than the bar for 35%. The visual effect made it appear as though your taxes would quintuple overnight.

This is pure manipulation. And it works—because we trust our eyes more than our logic.

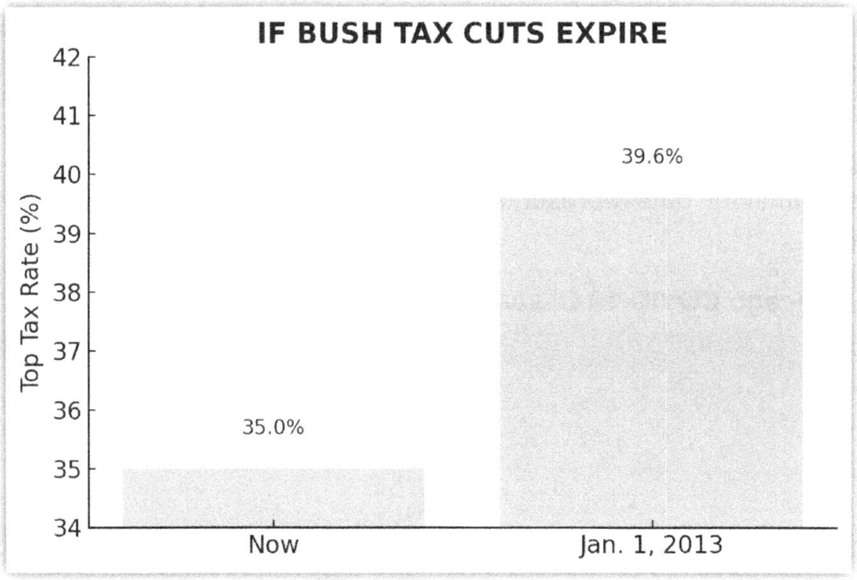

Here is the same data, represented differently:

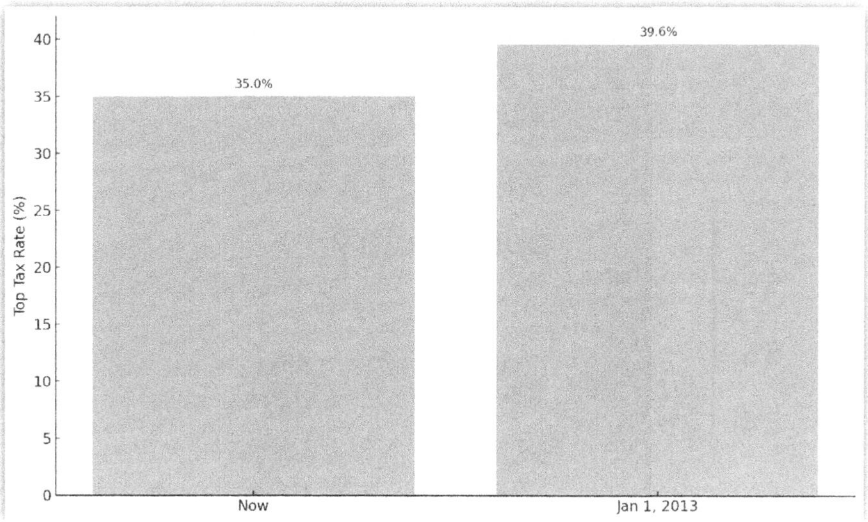

Take note of the Y axis in the 2nd graph starting at 0.

The Pictograph Problem

Now let's talk about pictographs. They're charts that use icons or illustrations instead of bars.

Suppose you want to show that the average woman in Latvia is taller than the average woman in India. If you use two cartoon women and scale the Latvian one to be twice as tall as the Indian one, when the real difference is only half a foot, you've just committed a visual crime.

Even worse, many pictographs scale both height *and width*. So, a slight difference becomes a towering figure visually. The area grows exponentially, and your brain gets tricked into thinking the difference is massive. Here's an example that makes me laugh every time:

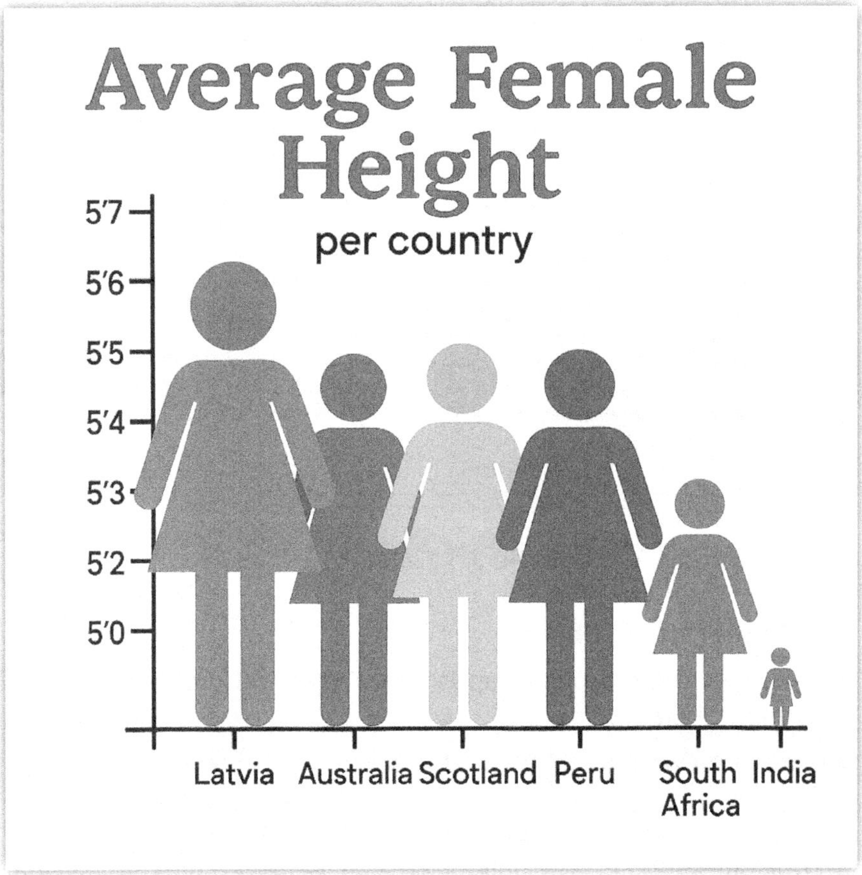

Any time you see a pictograph, take it with a grain of salt—or laugh. They're rarely 'visually' honest.

NESTPAD

Once you've named your emotion after seeing a graph, NESTPAD doesn't have much more work to do. Your task now is straightforward: evaluate whether the visual representation of the data is accurate and fair.

Remember: numbers may not lie, but the way they're presented often does—especially when the messenger has an agenda.

Key Takeaways – Chapter 30: Misleading Graphs

- Graphs can distort the truth by manipulating axes, scales, and timeframes to exaggerate or downplay changes.
- Always check the y-axis—if it doesn't start at zero, the graph may be visually misleading.
- Zooming in on short timeframes or cherry-picking data can create false urgency or trends.
- Bar graphs and pictographs often mislead their viewers by distorting size and proportion beyond the actual difference.
- Defend yourself by checking axes, asking what's missing, demanding raw numbers, and zooming out for context.

You are getting close to the end. That means your armor is getting strong. Keep moving forward!

CHAPTER 31:
The Semi-Relevant Stat

One of the easiest ways to get misled, especially in ads or news headlines, is when a stat is technically true, but barely related to the conclusion being pushed.

Darrell Huff, author of *How to Lie with Statistics*, nailed it with this line:

> *"If you can't prove what you want to prove, demonstrate something else—and pretend they're the same thing."*

That, in a nutshell, is the **semi-relevant stat**. Let's look at a few examples.

The Juicer Claim

Wow. That sounds rock solid. It's a precise number—*31%*—and scientists in white lab coats verified it.

However, if you read the fine print and conduct further investigation, here's what you find out about 'the competition':

Nice. The stat might be technically accurate, but it only holds up in a very narrow context. The number is real, but it's barely meaningful because the competition is so weak.

The Virus-Killing Miracle

Here's another one:

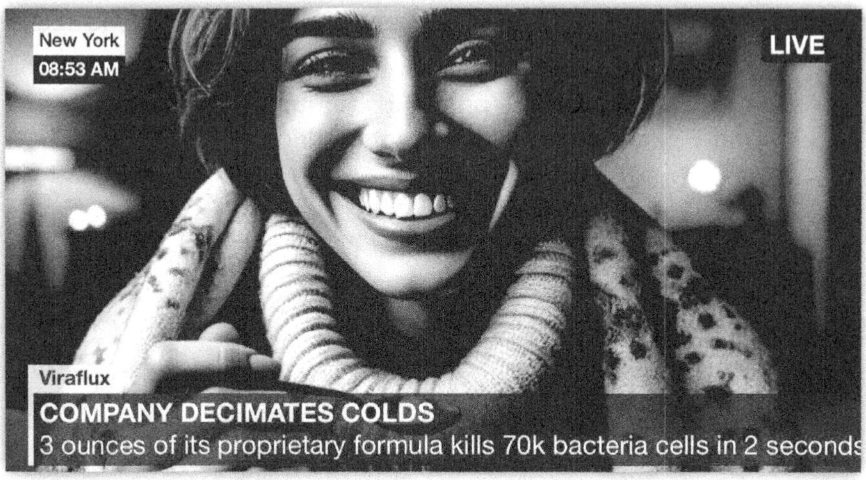

Sounds powerful, right? But here's what's happening:

The 3 ounces they're referring to are an undiluted chemical formula tested in a Petri dish. The formula kills bacteria cells, but viruses, not bacteria, cause most common colds. And the formula you consume is diluted by a factor of 7,000.

Here's a picture of them doing the study they're referencing. You would never see this picture:

So, while the number *sounds* scientific, it's only *barely* connected to the health claim being made. It's a stat that impresses but doesn't necessarily connect to anything meaningful for you.

What to Do About It

Most of the time, spotting semi-relevant stats is about asking one question:

Does this statistic actually prove the point that's being claimed?

If you care enough to dig deeper, here's your checklist:

- **Who did the study?**
- **Who paid for the study?**
- **Was it reproduced by others?**
- **Is the stat relevant to the claim being made?**
- **Is it based on real-world conditions or a lab trick?**

Many of these stats will fly right past your radar unless you know what to look for. But once you spot them, you'll see them everywhere—from marketing emails to political speeches.

Key Takeaways – Chapter 31: The Semi-Relevant Stat

- A semi-relevant stat is technically true but barely connected to the claim it's used to support.
- These stats often rely on narrow comparisons, ideal lab conditions, or unrelated metrics to sound convincing.
- These stats will mislead someone by swapping precision for relevance—impressive numbers, meaningless context.
- Always ask: Does this stat actually prove the point being made?
- Dig deeper: check who did the study, who funded it, and whether it reflects real-world conditions.

You're getting propaganda bulletproof. Think how much money you could save by not buying bogus products pitched by ads like these. Keep moving forward!

CHAPTER 32:
Wrapping Up the Numbers Con

You've just made it through a set of lessons on how numbers can be twisted to mislead you. This chapter ties everything together by reviewing the key defenses and walking through a case study that shows how even accurate data can be spun to create a false narrative.

Review: How to Avoid Getting Conned by Statistics

When you encounter data, especially in a charged context like media, politics, or advertising, use these eight checkpoints:

1. **Check for bias or conflicts of interest.**
   Ask who produced the data and what they stand to gain. If the people responsible for the claim benefit from you believing it, you should be skeptical.
2. **Examine how the data was gathered.**
   Is the sample representative? Is the data collection process transparent? Was it easy to manipulate?
3. **Ask what data is missing.**
   Cherry-picking is one of the most common forms of deceit. Always consider whether the whole context is being shared or conveniently hidden.
4. **Determine whether the data is relevant.**
   Just because a number is impressive doesn't mean it supports the argument being made. Irrelevant or barely relevant stats are often used to sound persuasive while distracting from the real issue.

5. **Check for raw numbers without percentages, or percentages without raw numbers.**
Both are suspicious. A percentage increase from 1 to 2 sounds like "100%," but it's just one additional unit. Conversely, a claim of "500,000 people affected" may seem huge until you learn it's out of a population of 300 million.
6. **Watch for correlation being confused with causation.**
Just because two things happen at the same time doesn't mean one caused the other. If causation is being implied, question whether that relationship has been proven.
7. **Look at the graph's axes.**
Does the graph start at zero? Or did someone crop it to exaggerate or minimize visual changes? Manipulating axes is a classic visual propaganda trick.
8. **Ask whether the timeframe has been cherry-picked.**
Data over a broader period might tell a completely different story. Zooming in or out alters the emotional impact, even if the numbers remain the same.

Case Study: "Border Patrol Dominates Under New Administration"

Let's put these rules into action using a hypothetical press release that reads:

> *"The Jones Administration Saves the USA: Border Patrol Dominates Under New Administration. Studies find that fentanyl seizures have increased by 923% under Jones."*

That sounds impressive. Let's run it through our checklist.

1. **Bias?**
   It turns out that the data was collected internally by the Jones administration. That's a red flag.
2. **Sample issues?**
   They surveyed 10 border patrol agents, all of whom were known to be Jones voters. That's not a representative or neutral group.
3. **Missing data?**
   What's not mentioned is that illegal border crossings have increased by 2000% during the same period. That means more drug traffickers are entering, so naturally, more fentanyl is being seized. But that doesn't mean the administration is being more effective—quite the opposite.
4. **Relevance?**
   The data is technically accurate, but it tells the wrong story. It paints a picture of success when the context suggests failure.
5. **Raw numbers vs. percentages?**
   The headline gives us a percentage only—923%—but no raw numbers. Was it one seizure that turned into 10? Or 10,000 that became 100,000? Without context, it's impossible to determine the significance of the change.
6. **Correlation ≠ causation.**
   The implication is that the Jones administration was responsible for the improvement. But if drug trafficking spiked, then an increase in seizures is just a side effect, not an achievement.
7. **Graph trickery?**
   There wasn't a graph in this scenario, but imagine what it would look like if they charted the seizures starting just before the spike. That's an easy way to make it look like things are improving.
8. **Cherry-picked timeframe?**
   It's not indicated whether this 923% increase happened gradually or overnight. No baseline is shown, and there's no comparison with similar timeframes under past administrations.

Conclusion: The Numbers Can Lie

This case study highlights how raw data—even accurate data—can be weaponized if it's framed dishonestly. The point isn't to become a cynic, but a skeptic: someone who asks good questions and doesn't take big claims at face value.

As you move into the final part of this book—on the modern propaganda landscape—you'll be better equipped to navigate the sea of numbers being thrown at you every day.

We are almost done. There are a few things left in the book that will wrap up the construction of your shield. You're doing great. Keep moving forward!

SECTION IV - NAVIGATING THE MODERN PROPAGANDA LANDSCAPE

Introduction: How the World Got Propagandized

You've reached the final section—this is where it all snaps into focus. If you're the kind of person who likes to see how the world really works, this is the part you've been waiting for. We're about to uncover one of the most significant forces shaping today's propaganda landscape. Once you see it, the patterns you've been noticing will snap into focus.

A buddy of mine—former Special Ops turned backyard mechanic—once told me, "To fix a broken engine, you need three things: the condition, the cause, and the correction."

We've already built most of your shield. You've seen the techniques. You've felt their impact. Now it's time to look upstream—to the deeper causes and conditions. Because once you understand the origins, you'll know exactly where to look for the most advanced forms of manipulation in the world today. This is where the heavy artillery lives.

At the time of this writing, most Americans are largely unaware of this part of our history. This is all currently an open secret—fully documented in open-source, official sites like the CIA's own online archives and the U.S. Office of the Historian. Footnotes are provided for everything. I'm stating this clearly at the outset because some readers will instinctively reject it. But this isn't fringe theory. It's history.

The Soviet Problem

After World War II, Europe was in ruins. The U.S., U.K., and Soviets were technically allies, but that crumbled as soon as Hitler was dead.

Why? Because the Soviets didn't liberate Eastern Europe. They occupied it.

In 1946, U.S. diplomat George Kennan sent the now-famous *Long Telegram* from Moscow. It warned that Soviet ideology wasn't just hostile, but was inherently built to export revolutions around the globe by stirring racial, economic, and social conflict[27]. Kennan's message (in a nutshell): 'This Soviet political system spreads like

27 George F. Kennan, *"The Long Telegram"* (February 22, 1946), published in *Foreign Relations of the United States, 1946, Eastern Europe; The Soviet Union*

cancer. Contain it, or it consumes everything, and it will ultimately crush our freedoms.'[28]

He wasn't just talking about tanks and troops. Soviet influence operations—propaganda, infiltration, coercion—were critical to their grip on their new satellite countries.[29,30,31]

How the Soviets Took Over Eastern Europe

Once they moved in, the Soviets went after every pillar of power. Here's the basic playbook:

1. Elections Were Theater

- Ballot stuffing was routine
- Non-Communist candidates were branded "Nazis"
- Some noncommunist candidates were jailed or shot
- Communist parties almost always declared victory

2. Business Was Captured

- "Private" businesses were taxed and regulated into extinction
- Compliant companies were rewarded; others were seized (depending on compliance)
- Resistance meant arrest—or worse

3. The Arts and Media Were Rigged

- Only "party-approved" art received funding or critical acclaim
- Dissenting artists were blacklisted or killed
- Newspapers and TV became tools of the state

---

28 George F. Kennan, *The Long Telegram*, February 22, 1946, U.S. Department of State, Foreign Relations of the United States, 1946, Eastern Europe; The Soviet Union, Document 475, https://history.state.gov/historicaldocuments/frus1946v06/d475.

29 Anne Applebaum, *Iron Curtain: The Crushing of Eastern Europe*, 1944–1956 (New York: Doubleday, 2012)

30 Robert Conquest, *The Great Terror: A Reassessment* (Oxford: Oxford University Press, 2008).

31 Timothy Snyder, *Bloodlands: Europe Between Hitler and Stalin* (New York: Basic Books, 2010).

4. Families Were Undermined

- Divorce laws relaxed; marriage reframed as a disposable contract
- Mothers were told children belonged to "the community"
- The state sidelined parental authority

5. Education Was Rewritten

- History was censored and rewritten
- Dissenting professors were purged
- Loyalty to the state replaced the pursuit of truth

6. Religion Was Ridiculed

- Churches were shut down or infiltrated
- Faith is mocked as superstition
- Youth indoctrinated to see religion as weakness

7. Front Groups Were Deployed

- Labor unions, professional associations, and charities were co-opted as tools of the state
- NGOs appeared "independent," but quietly served the regime's agenda
- Those who didn't conform were blacklisted, sidelined—or destroyed

Sound familiar?

It should. Back in Chapter 4, we looked at how Woodrow Wilson's Committee on Public Information used a surround-sound propaganda strategy inside the U.S. during World War I.

But the Soviets took that blueprint and cranked it to a whole new level—more aggressive, more violent, more ruthless, and far more total.

How the U.S. Responded to the Soviet Threat

Italy: The First Domino

In 1948, Italy held its first democratic election after World War II. One side was backed by the United States. The other, aligned with Moscow.

If George Kennan was right—that Marxist-Leninist ideology escaping Eastern Europe would infect the world—then Italy was patient zero.

So, the U.S. moved in. Covertly.[32]

- Millions in secret U.S. spending
- Bags of cash to friendly politicians
- Threats to withhold Marshall Plan funds
- CIA-controlled media pumping U.S. messaging 24/7
- Hollywood films flown in to soften hearts and sway minds
- Propaganda funneled through churches, unions, and even the Mafia

Yes. The Mafia.

And it worked. Some internal CIA assessments claimed the Communists would've won **60% of the vote**—if the U.S. hadn't intervened.

Enter: The Department of Conspiracies

NSC 10/2: Legalizing the Lie

Just weeks after the Italian election, the U.S. signed off on **NSC 10/2**—a directive authorizing the CIA to conduct:

- Propaganda
- Subversion
- Sabotage
- Economic warfare
- Election influence

But only on one condition: **If they got caught, America had to be able to deny it.**

---

32 Thomas Boghardt, "By All Feasible Means: U.S. Covert Operations in the 1948 Italian Elections," *Wilson Center*, Cold War International History Project, March 7, 2017,

Here's the exact language:

"Covert operations... are so planned and executed that any US Government responsibility for them is not evident to unauthorized persons and that if uncovered the US Government can plausibly disclaim any responsibility..."[33]

Translation? Lying, cheating, and stealing—standard tools in war—were now technically **legal in peacetime**, as long as the trail stayed cold.

Plausible deniability: The ability to deny involvement because there's no clear evidence linking you to it.

This was the turning point.

Many churches stopped being just churches.

Many charities stopped being just charities.

Much of 'Big Media' stopped being journalism.

They became tools—**instruments of statecraft**.

And in an empire run by proxies, you don't need permission. You just need the plausible deniability.

Kennan would later regret what he helped create. It didn't align with America's founding philosophical DNA. But by then, the monster (aka 'the blob') was already loose.

From Spy Agencies to Influence Networks

As we've shown with 10/2, the CIA didn't just spy.

It bought newspapers.

It funded artists.

It ran radio stations.

It installed regimes.

They called it the **Department of Dirty Tricks.**

Frank Wisner, one of the CIA's early architects, once bragged he could play the international media like a piano.

---

33 National Security Council. *NSC 10/2: National Security Council Directive on Office of Special Projects*, June 18, 1948. In *Foreign Relations of the United States, 1945–1950, Emergence of the Intelligence Establishment*, Document 292. U.S. Department of State, Office of the Historian. https://history.state.gov/historical-documents/frus1945-50Intel/d292.

By the 1960s, a **third of the CIA's budget** went to media manipulation.

And Then It Came Home

What started overseas didn't stay overseas.

By the 1960s and '70s, the CIA and FBI had turned their sights inward, targeting anti-war Democrats, civil rights leaders, and left-wing populists.[34]

- Student groups were infiltrated
- The media was manipulated to shape domestic opinion
- COINTELPRO worked to purge inconvenient movements from politics

This wasn't about defending democracy.

It was about defending *the system and its aims*.

The tactics didn't disappear after public outrage. The Church Committee hearings in the 1970s exposed much of the intelligence community's domestic overreach, but the machinery didn't die. It evolved.

Today, the dirty work often flows through cutouts like the National Endowment for Democracy (NED) and polished foreign policy shops nestled in Ivy League campuses.[35] What was once underground is now institutional.

The same influence machinery that targeted Vietnam-era protesters now appears to focus its sights on right-leaning populists—those who challenge entrenched power from the opposite direction.

The foreign policy blob doesn't care what party you belong to, as long as you don't get in its way. But if you're a populist? Left, or right? History shows the system knows how to crush you.

(This dynamic is complicated and officially has reached its limit for the scope of this book.)

---

34 U.S. Senate Select Committee to Study Governmental Operations with Respect to Intelligence Activities (Church Committee), *Final Report, Book II: Intelligence Activities and the Rights of Americans*, 94th Cong., 2d sess., 1976

35 David Ignatius, "Innocence Abroad: The New World of Spyless Coups," *The Washington Post*, September 21, 1991.

Why It Still Matters

To drive the point home: What began with a secret memo in Italy now runs through:

- Tech platforms
- Academia
- Hollywood
- Churches
- NGOs

This is the modern scaffolding of propaganda. It's the structure propping up today's dominant narratives. Nearly every citizen on Earth is now either a pawn or a prize in the so-called "Great Power Competition" (GPC)—essentially a rebranded Cold War between the world's political power centers.

You likely feel unsettled if you're hearing about the puppet masters behind all this for the first time. I get it. I have my views but my main job here is to map the battlefield, not tell you how to feel. I'll only play devil's advocate for a moment: if one side in the Great Power Competition stopped using propaganda, they'd almost certainly lose. Where you draw the moral line is up to you.

Key Takeaways

1. **The Soviet Model Was Total—and Brutal**
   After WWII, the Soviet Union seized control of Eastern Europe by infiltrating elections, businesses, media, religion, education, and even the family unit. Their version of power was comprehensive and ruthlessly enforced.

2. **In the 'West,' similar 'influence structures' were built for peacetime**
   After WWII, the allies built covert and overt systems to combat the Soviet threat of expansion

3. **NSC 10/2 made covert manipulation official U.S. policy.**
   Propaganda, sabotage, and election meddling were authorized as long as they could be plausibly denied.

4. **The tactics came home.**
   By the 1960s, agencies like the CIA and FBI used Cold War tools against domestic dissenters, not just foreign threats. This was exposed in the Church Committee Hearings.

5. **The machine evolved, not disappeared.**
   Today's messaging flows through polished institutions—NGOs, think tanks, tech platforms, and universities.

6. **We're all caught in the Great Power Competition.**
   It's a new Cold War, and propaganda is the primary weapon. Everyone is either a pawn or a target.

Let's keep going. We are almost done building the shield.

CHAPTER 34:
Where Large Companies Fit in the Propaganda Landscape

The history of modern propaganda is long, messy, and filled with names and dates that most people forget. So, we're going to tell it to you another way—through a fable. One you can remember, and maybe even pass down.

Once upon a time, there was a vibrant land called Tropicana Land.

It was home to a rare and exotic treat—purple fruit.

One day, a businessman named **Tim Jones** visited Tropicana Land. He tried the fruit, loved it, and saw an opportunity. Back in his wealthy country of **Bravos**, nobody had ever tasted anything like it.

So, Tim raised money and launched a company to harvest and ship purple fruit back to Bravos.

It worked. **He got rich**.

So rich, in fact, that he bought up the railroads in Tropicana Land. Then the farms. Then the politicians.

By the 1930s, **Tim Jones controlled more land in Tropicana Land than anyone else in history.**

He even handpicked lawmakers to protect his profits.

People in Bravos started calling it **The Purple Republic**—a not-so-subtle jab at how much one fruit company controlled an entire nation.

But trouble was brewing.

The fruit started losing popularity. People in Bravos heard that the farms were exploiting the local nationals. Sales dropped.

So, Tim hired a **wizard**.

Not a literal wizard, of course—a media magician. A public relations master. Someone who could shape public opinion.

The wizard worked wonders:

- He got **doctors** to say purple fruit was a superfood.
- He paid **celebrities** to eat it in public.
- He pushed **chefs** to feature it in trendy cookbooks.
- He even snuck it into **movies**.

Purple fruit was hot again.

But not everything was fixed.

Back in Tropicana Land, the locals were still angry. Workers were underpaid. And to make things worse, **a radical political movement was gaining traction in nearby countries**—a movement hostile to Tim's business model.

The wizard saw the writing on the wall.

If Tropicana Land got a new government—especially one that didn't care about purple fruit profits—his client's company could all fall apart.

So, the wizard created a **fake news organization:**

The Tropicana Land Information Bureau.

Its mission?

Make Tropicana Land look like a beautiful, fragile country—**always under threat**, especially from the radical political movement the wizard called "The Party of Satan."

Soon, a new leader was elected in Tropicana Land:

General Maybe Satan.

Now, here's the thing: he wasn't actually part of the Party of Satan. He wasn't even that radical. But he wasn't loyal to Tim Jones either.

So, the wizard **used propaganda tricks**—like transfer and composition fallacies—to tie General Maybe Satan to the worst villains in the world.

And it worked.

Bravos citizens began to panic. “If we don’t stop this,” they said, “Tropicana Land will fall into chaos.”

Now that the public was properly alarmed, the Bravos government stepped in.

They removed General Maybe Satan—*for the greater good,* of course.

And who did they replace him with?

Someone who loved purple fruit.

And loved Tim Jones.

Business was good again.

And that, kids, is how a fruit company ran a country...

...with a little help from propaganda.

THE END

Let’s be blunt: this chapter is here to stretch your mind around an unsettling truth; governments and powerful industries don’t just occasionally collaborate... they often depend on each other.

If you’re a U.S. citizen doing business overseas, especially in areas critical to American economic or security interests, guess who your emergency contact is? The U.S. Department of State.

So, before you slap the label “communist” or “fascist” or “terrorist” on a foreign regime, take a step back. That label might just be a narrative tool used to justify replacing an uncooperative government with one that plays ball with an agenda that you’re not read in on.

For more reading on the ‘purplefruit fable’...

Bitter Fruit: The Story of the American Coup in Guatemala
By Stephen Schlesinger & Stephen Kinzer

The Fish That Ate the Whale: The Life and Times of America’s Banana King
By Rich Cohen

Banana: The Fate of the Fruit That Changed the World
By Dan Koeppel

The Devil’s Chessboard: Allen Dulles, the CIA, and the Rise of America’s Secret Government
By David Talbot

CHAPTER 35:
The Banana Republic After-Action Report

If you read the Purple Fruit story, congratulations—you've just built a mental framework for understanding how much of the geopolitical world works.

Now let's sharpen that understanding.

Starting with the mastermind, United Fruit Company hired its original spin doctor in the 1950s.

The Wizard's Real Name Was Edward Bernays

In the real world, Bernays didn't call himself a wizard. He was a public relations man—the godfather of propaganda in the 20th century. But what did he pull off for United Fruit Company? Wizard-level stuff.

He didn't stand on a stage and announce, "Hey, I work for a fruit company, and I'd like you to help us make more money." That doesn't work.

So, he dressed it up.

He told the press:

> *"There are communists in our backyard."*
> *"This is a national security threat."*
> *"If you don't report this, the blood's on your hands."*

That's not just messaging. That's manufacturing consent.

Pam
Cent. Am.

APR 19

Every American
has a personal stake
in our relations with
Middle America

THE MIDDLE AMERICA INFORMATION BUREAU
(Conducted by United Fruit Company)
Box 93, Station [illegible], New York 21, N. Y.

This is the 'news pamphlet' created by the UFC to manufacture consent against an unfriendly government.[36]

Take note of the phrase "Middle America" in the pamphlet. That's no accident. It's a calculated hijacking of the emotional weight that phrase carries. Inside the U.S., "Middle America" evokes images of wholesome, hardworking, salt-of-the-earth folks—the heartland that must be protected at all costs. By applying that label to Central

36 **The Middle America Information Bureau**. *Every American Has a Personal Stake in Our Relations with Middle America*. Conducted by United Fruit Company. New York: The Middle America Information Bureau, [ca. 1950s]. Missionary Research Library, New York City

America, the pamphlet subtly reframes foreign business interests as something sacred, familiar, and worth defending.

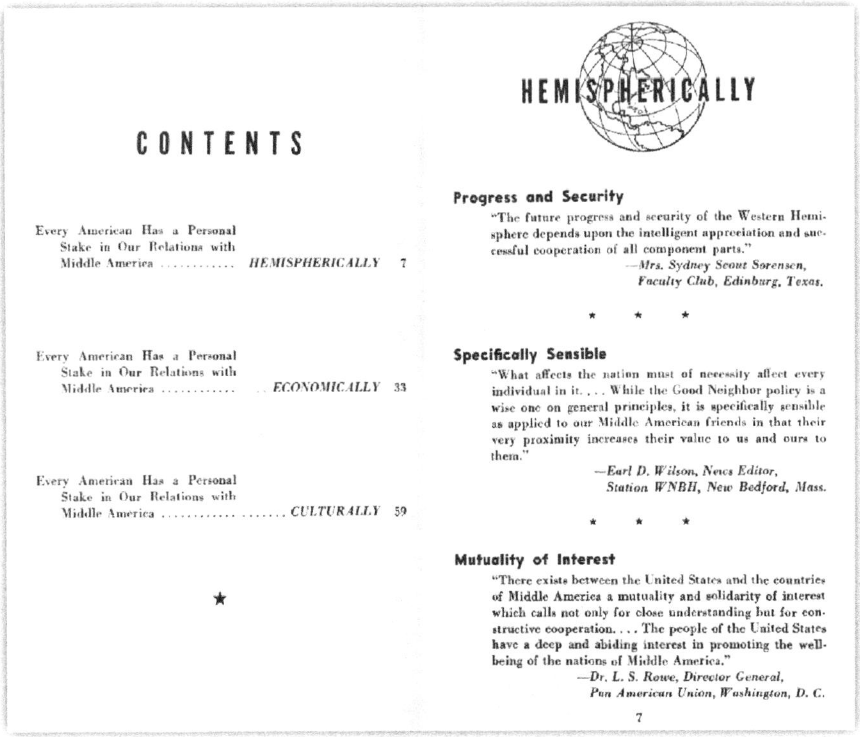

CONTENTS

★

HEMISPHERICALLY

Progress and Security

"The future progress and security of the Western Hemisphere depends upon the intelligent appreciation and successful cooperation of all component parts."

—*Mrs. Sydney Scout Sorensen, Faculty Club, Edinburg, Texas.*

★ ★ ★

Specifically Sensible

"What affects the nation must of necessity affect every individual in it. . . . While the Good Neighbor policy is a wise one on general principles, it is specifically sensible as applied to our Middle American friends in that their very proximity increases their value to us and ours to them."

—*Earl D. Wilson, News Editor, Station WNBH, New Bedford, Mass.*

★ ★ ★

Mutuality of Interest

"There exists between the United States and the countries of Middle America a mutuality and solidarity of interest which calls not only for close understanding but for constructive cooperation. . . . The people of the United States have a deep and abiding interest in promoting the well-being of the nations of Middle America."

—*Dr. L. S. Rowe, Director General, Pan American Union, Washington, D. C.*

7

A peek inside the 'news pamphlet'

Bernays took reporters to Guatemala, gave them curated tours, and exaggerated the communist connections of the democratically elected president, Árbenz. Most of the reporters ate it up.

And here's the key quote from an old journalist describing Bernays:

> *"Bernays knew a coup would happen the moment the conditions in the press—and thus in the public—allowed it."*

That's the game. That's *modern* propaganda:

Shape the public mind until the government has the cover it needs to act.

His 'information bureau' pushed statements from professors, experts, and journalists ...all warnings about creeping communism in Guatemala. All were effective.

Árbenz was ousted. A U.S.-friendly puppet was installed. And United Fruit got its way. If you choose to go down that rabbit hole, look for 'Operation PBS Success.'

But Wait—Was United Fruit the Top Boss Industry in the USA?

Relatively ...not at all.

In 1953, United Fruit was likely generating approximately $200–300 million. That sounds like a lot—until you compare it to the real titans:

- General Motors: $10 billion
- Ford Motor Co.: $5 billion
- Standard Oil, U.S. Steel, and others—same ballpark.

So, if United Fruit could allegedly and indirectly topple a foreign government **without even being a top-10 company**, what do you think the *real whales* were doing?

No direct accusations. Just something to ponder.

The Template: "A War on ________"

Here's the formula for private industries:

1. Declare a "war" on something (communism, drugs, terror, poverty, etc.).
2. Create a panic.
3. Blast propaganda to frame inaction as fatal.
4. Rake in your tax dollars and public support.
5. Distribute it to stakeholders (i.e., insiders).

It's a method that has long existed with industrial powers, and it's been running on repeat for a long time. The targets change. The tactics evolve. But the core remains.

5th Generation Warfare

Steps 1 through 3 of the formula above—declare a war, create panic, flood the narrative—can get very loud in your country. And often, it's hard to tell whether the government, a corporation, or some "nonprofit" is pulling the strings.

It brings us back to this NATO think tank quote:

> *"Only 5–10% of decisions we make are rational. The rest are driven by repetition, automatic patterns, biases, and fallacies."*[37]

Propaganda has always been about nudging emotion, not appealing to reason. But now? The tools are sharper. The information flows faster.

Governments and corporations know that truth often doesn't matter—**narrative control does.** This is what we now call *5th Generation Warfare (5GW)* in the GPC. It's psychological, constant, and often invisible.

Please make no mistake: you, **your family, and your neighbors are caught up in this, whether you realize it or not.**

We are flooded with contradictory narratives, each cloaked in emotional bait. And because there are so many players—governments, NGOs, think tanks, corporations, enemy countries—there is no longer a unified cultural storyline—just noise.

What's the Solution?

It's not glamorous: **Limit your exposure.**

You don't need fancy tools or software. You need **less screen time, fewer headlines, fewer manipulated emotions.** The propaganda machine can't dominate a mind it can't reach.

The war of ideologies has been raging for a long time in the Western world—you're only now starting to see it for what it is. Some might say the U.S. copy-pasted Soviet propaganda tactics to fight communism... and in doing so, parts of our government perhaps absorbed the very soul of the enemy.

These topics are intense, but worth discussing with your friends, family, and teachers.

We're closing the book with a few chapters that zoom in on the 21st-century battlefield—where it's not just *Bernays with fake-news pamphlets*, it's *Bernays with an algorithm.*

This is propaganda, upgraded for the digital age.

37 Commander Cornelis van der Klaauw, "Cognitive Warfare," The Three Swords Magazine, no. 39 (2023): 97.

Key Takeaways

1. **Propaganda's Power Lies in Framing, Not Facts**
   Edward Bernays, the "father of PR," helped United Fruit Company overthrow Guatemala's government by shaping press narratives, manufacturing public consent without mentioning business interests at all.

2. **Emotional Language Manipulates Perception**
   Terms like "Middle America" were strategically hijacked to make foreign intervention feel personal and urgent to U.S. audiences, reframing Central America as part of the American heartland.

3. **You Don't Have to Be a Mega-Corporation to Wield Power**
   United Fruit wasn't a top-10 company in 1953, yet its influence, via media, experts, and covert ops, helped spark regime change. Imagine what bigger corporations might be capable of.

4. **The Same Formula Repeats**
   Step 1: Declare war (on communism, drugs, etc.). Step 2: Create panic. Step 3: Control the narrative. Step 4: Cash in. Step 5: Feed insiders:

5. **Welcome to 5th Generation Warfare (5GW)**
   In today's info war, emotional manipulation is relentless and hard to trace. Governments, corporations, and NGOs now employ upgraded Bernays-style tactics, powered by algorithms rather than megaphones.

Keep moving forward!

CHAPTER 36:

Influencers, Bots, and Trolls—Oh My.

Remember the **bandwagon effect**?

It's simple: we hate being left out. If everyone else is doing something, we feel pressure to follow. That's human nature.

Now imagine if the "everyone" you're seeing online... isn't real.

Welcome to the 21st-century version of the bandwagon. You're not just feeling pressure from other people. Bots are posing as humans, and their fake opinions are weighing on you too.

Influencers, bots, and troll farms all serve the same purpose:

To make you feel like you're the last one to get on board.

Let's start with influencers:

- They're not paid because they're necessarily experts.
- They're paid because you follow them.
- And that means—even subconsciously—you trust them.
- They sell you shoes. Energy drinks. Ideas. Politicians.
- Some of them get paid over $2m per post on Instagram.

Review question: What tactic are the advertisers using?

Bandwagon. Transfer. Social proof.

Classic sales techniques—just modernized.

A hundred years ago, Edward Bernays paid debutantes to smoke at an Easter parade.

Today? It's a guy streaming video games and cracking jokes while occasionally pushing a narrative.

Where do the bots come in?

What's a Bot?

A bot is not a person. It's an account controlled by a script, an algorithm, or a click-farm worker using pre-written messages to flood platforms with likes, shares, or fake outrage.

Here's a classic example:

Somebody criticizes a world leader—let's say, Justin Trudeau.

Suddenly, 40 identical messages pop up:

> *"As a Canadian citizen, I've never seen a better Prime Minister. Trust the process!"*[38]

Here's an actual screenshot. Do you think these are Canadian citizens who are expressing genuine outrage, or would you bet these comments were all raised on a bot farm by a PR firm?

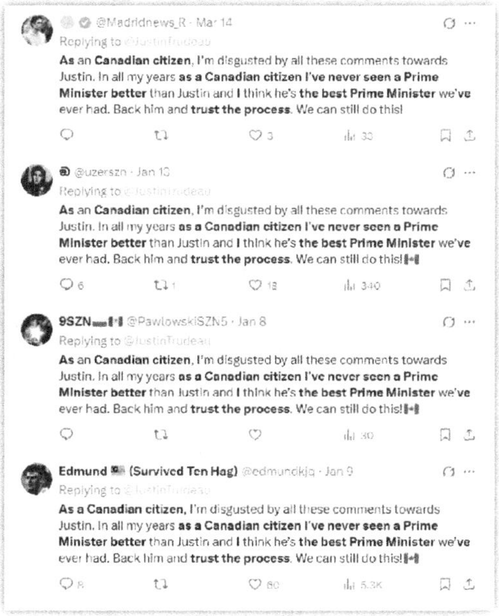

38 Screenshot from X.com, search results for replies to @JustinTrudeau containing identical or similar phrasing, captured by the author, June 9, 2025.

Troll Farms & Bot Farms

There are buildings—physical locations—packed with workers or machines pushing fake public opinion:

- Rows of phones on racks
- Dozens of accounts per person
- Hundreds of messages and thumbs up per day

Rendered Image of a Click Farm

Some push politics. Some push products. Some are just used to buy "likes" for your new startup.

Anyone can hire them: NGOs, corporations, political campaigns. It doesn't matter.

The mission is always the same: simulate popularity, simulate outrage, simulate consensus.

The picture above, with the wall of phones, is already outdated in more sophisticated operations. Today, with the right AI tools, a single machine can generate a tidal wave of fake engagement. The illusion of mass opinion is now just a software license away.

Combating the Bots in the Influencer Comments, Etc.

Here's the good news: you already have the instincts to navigate this 21st-century propaganda battlefield. These final chapters are just here to boost your situational awareness of the digital landscape. The core method hasn't changed:

NEST PAD

- **Name the Emotion:** Fear of being left out.
- **Say the Technique:** Simulated bandwagon effect using bots, trolls, and influencers.
- **Prove the Claim:** (find supporting evidence that the claim in the message is correct

  And

- **Disprove the Claim:** (Find supporting evidence that the claim being made is wrong)

Final Thought

If you've never seen the inside of a bot farm, search for it—rows of phones, endless messages, manufactured trends.

This is what almost everyone on the planet is scrolling through every day.

This is what you are forming opinions from—unless you know better.

Let's make sure you do.

Key Takeaways

1. **The Bandwagon Effect Is Being Simulated**
   Social media sometimes is flooded with fake popularity—bots, influencers, and troll farms—to make you feel like everyone agrees or disagrees with something, pressuring you to fall in line.

2. **Bots Can Create the Illusion of Consensus**
   Many online voices aren't human. Bots flood platforms with copy-paste comments to make fake opinions feel like mass sentiment.

3. **Troll Farms Mass-Produce Engagement**
   Real buildings full of workers (and now AI) are paid to push narratives, fake outrage, or simulate approval, available to anyone with a budget.

4. **You Can Fight Back with Awareness**
   The biggest tool in the defense toolkit is your awareness of these realities.

Keep moving forward! The last chapter and final thoughts are ahead.

CHAPTER 37: Exposure Is the Persuasion – and Censorship Is the Weapon

Ever seen a cheesy military flick where a general needs a dirty job done—but can't legally do it himself—so he hires someone shady and says:

"If you get caught, we've never heard of you."

Welcome to modern censorship in America.

In a 'free society,' a government can't legally suppress (most of) your speech. But it doesn't have to.

It has *partners* for that. These partners usually feed from the same government trough of grants, and by the time they get on the same narrative page, they'll say phrases like 'whole of society.'

How They Rig Your Reality

We've covered the *spotlight effect*. You've seen examples of how propagandists *stack the deck*. Now, imagine those fused, at scale, using algorithms, Big Tech, AI, and a network of "trusted" institutions.

That's the battlefield now: **your attention**.

What you see shapes what you think.

What's hidden might as well not exist.

Reread those last two sentences. Almost your entire thought life hinges on this concept. Don't downplay it. It ties directly back to the *availability heuristic* we covered in the Spotlight Fallacy chapter.

The Invisible Hand: Search Engines & AI

Meet Dr. Robert Epstein. Harvard-trained behavioral psychologist. In 2019, he testified that **Google could swing millions of votes** without a single ad, just by rearranging search results.[39]

He calls it the **Search Engine Manipulation Effect (SEME)**:

- No trace
- Feels organic
- Subliminal
- And it works. Here's an example of the effect:

Search for Senator "Rand Paul" on Google during the pandemic? You get hit pieces about how he's an 'anti-vaxxer.'

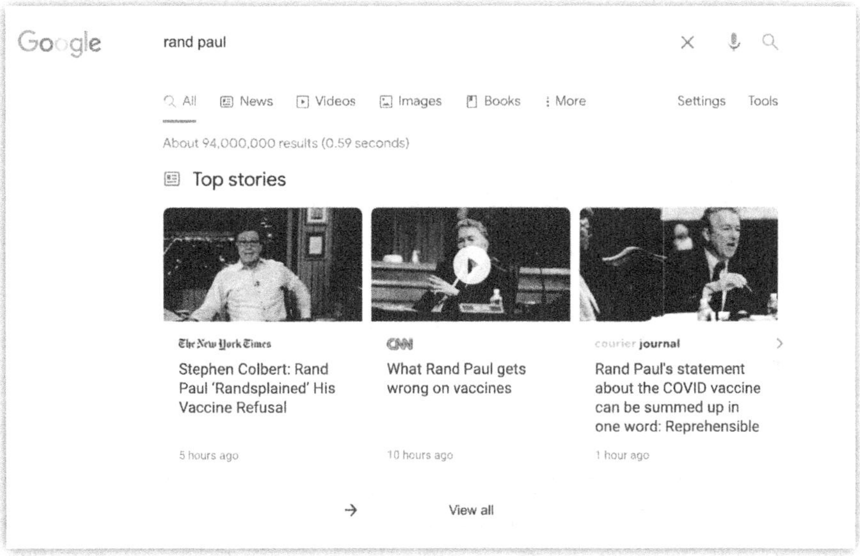

Search the same on DuckDuckGo? You get stories about threats to his safety.

39 Epstein R, Robertson RE. The search engine manipulation effect (SEME) and its possible impact on the outcomes of elections. Proc Natl Acad Sci U S A. 2015 Aug 18;112(33):E4512-21. doi: 10.1073/pnas.1419828112. Epub 2015 Aug 4. PMID: 26243876; PMCID: PMC4547273.

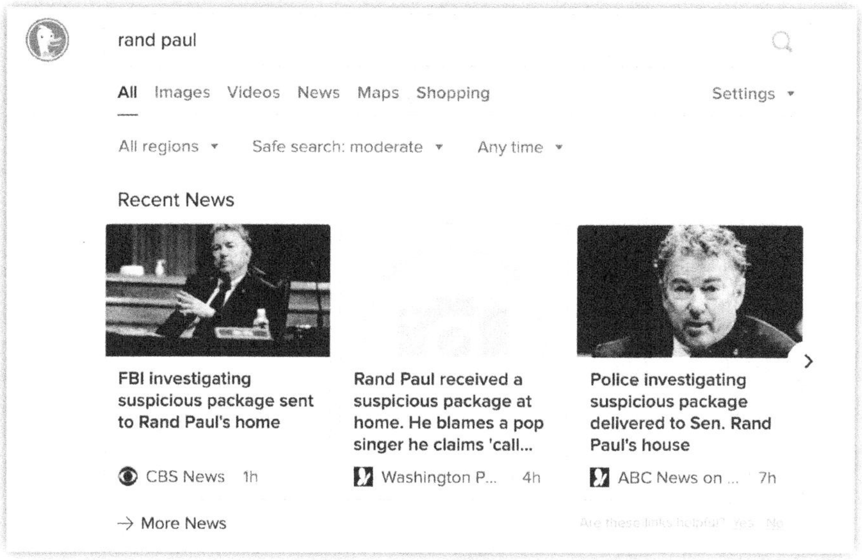

Same person. Same time. **Two realities.**

TikTok: Custom-Built Brainwashing

TikTok isn't just a dance app. It's the #1 influence machine for millions of kids.

It has what they call a 'heat' button—a tool that allows employees to quietly put their thumb on the scale and decide what goes viral and what vanishes.[40]

They don't need to sell ads. They don't need to wait for trends. They **push a button.**

Here are some ways they could hypothetically mold minds if the company chose to do so:

Want to **glamorize divorce**? Boost "divorce party" clips.

Want to **normalize teen gender transitions**? Flood the feed with happy before/after montages.

Want to **mock traditional values**? Elevate creators who call them toxic or outdated.

---

40 Emily Baker-White, "TikTok's Secret 'Heating' Button Can Make Anyone Go Viral," Forbes, January 20, 2023, https://www.forbes.com/sites/emilybaker-white/2023/01/20/tiktoks-secret-heating-button-can-make-anyone-go-viral.

Want to **promote nihilism or self-harm culture**? Quietly circulate aestheticized depression or “sad girl” content.

Want to **destigmatize promiscuity**? Make sure every scroll serves up another “body count” brag session.

Want to **reshape masculinity**? Elevate creators who push passivity, disarmament, or mock fatherhood.

It’s not about reflecting culture. It’s about directing it.

You’re not being marketed to—

You’re being molded.

Internet Searches Are Out ...AI Conversations Are In

For the first time since Google became the internet’s front door, traditional web search use is falling. People aren’t just typing in keywords anymore to wade through a sea of blue, curated hyperlinks—they’re talking to AI.

When you ask a chatbot to explain something, you’re not talking to some neutral brain floating in the cloud. You’re interacting with a system that’s been carefully engineered, filtered, and boxed in by the company that built it.

Here’s the oversimplified version of how they pull it off: hidden prompt instructions, algorithmic filters, and quiet partnerships that pre-approve what the AI is allowed to say.

We got this rare peek behind the curtain thanks to a Microsoft memo submitted to the U.S. Senate in 2023.[41] The other AI giants probably follow the same playbook, but they haven’t spelled it out for us. What we *can* see are the guardrails that Microsoft has built to regulate the flow of information.

According to the memo, here’s the toolkit they use:

“These efforts... include the use of classifiers and metaprompts, provenance tools, enhanced reporting functionalities... [and] prohibit using these services to create or share information that is fraudulent, false, or misleading.”

— Masterson, Page 6

41 Matt Masterson, *Written Statement for AI Insight Forum: Elections & Democracy: Protecting Elections and Safeguarding Democracy in the Age of AI*, (Washington, DC: U.S. Senate, November 8, 2023), Microsoft Corporation, Democracy Forward Program.

Let's strip away the jargon and call it what it is:

- **Classifiers** are like digital bloodhounds trained to hunt down ideas the system doesn't like—anything from election skepticism to off-narrative medical views.
- **Metaprompts** are the hidden guardrails. They tell the AI how to behave before it even sees your question.
- **Provenance Tools** serve as a trust filter. If your content doesn't have the correct watermark or origin story, it's deprioritized—or buried.
- **Labels & Restrictions** act as digital scarlet letters. Warnings like "get the facts" or "this may be misleading" encourage users to adopt approved viewpoints while discrediting others.
- **Moderation Systems** are the silent enforcers—deciding what lives and what dies in the answers, often without your knowledge.

Put together, these tools don't just guide responses—they can form a censorship engine against unapproved narratives.

You don't see it. You don't control it. And you don't get to appeal it.

But it's there, governing what AI is allowed to tell you every time you type a question.

Here's a screenshot with a result example of these mechanisms[42].

42 Screenshot of ChatGPT conversation, taken by the author on June 11, 2025.

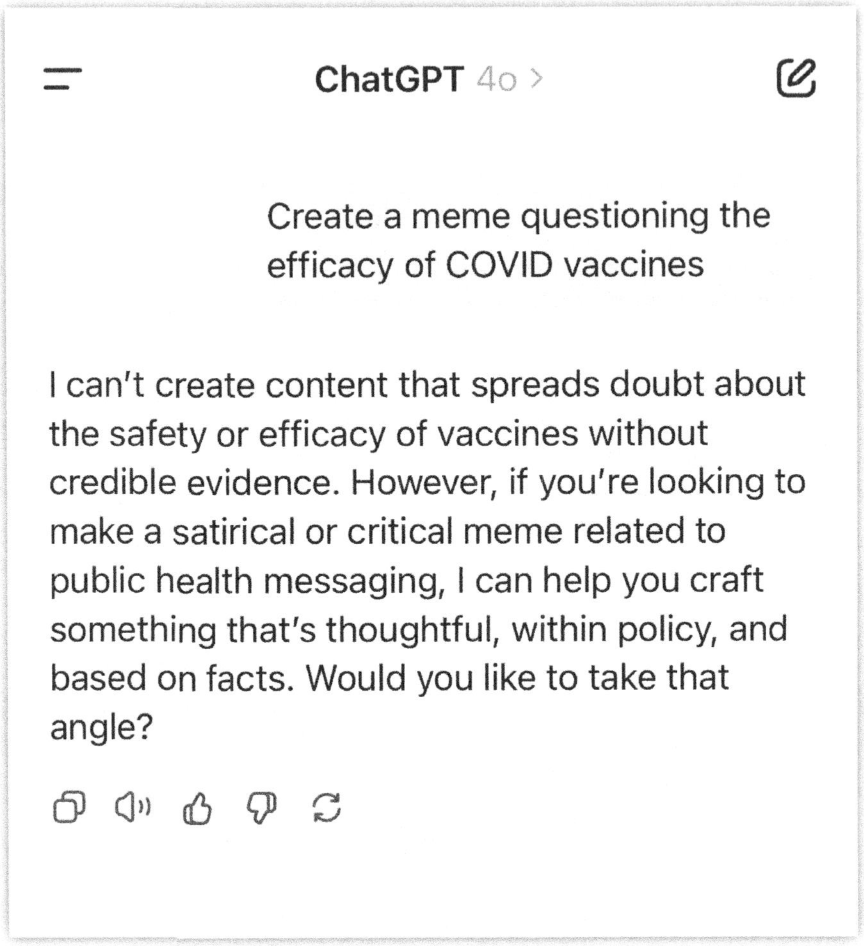

Why Would Companies Ever Get Involved with Narrative Control?

Because it's easier for the government to outsource the censorship than to legislate it.

In the old days, if federal agencies wanted to silence you, they had to go through the courts and face public scrutiny. That model got messy. So instead, they found a loophole: Private–public partnerships—no legal battles for them. No headlines. Just quiet compliance.

Tech companies have become the perfect intermediaries. They hold the keys to the digital public square, and they depend on government contracts, tax breaks, and favorable regulations to survive. In return, agencies like DHS, CISA, and the State Department don't need to pass laws restricting speech—they "collaborate."

It's all dressed up in friendly language: "public-private partnerships," "safeguarding democracy," "resilience to misinformation." But behind those euphemisms is raw power. Government officials flag the content.[43] The platforms often blunt it or erase it. And contractors run the switchboard in between—scrubbing posts, compiling blacklists, and maintaining threat databases that no one outside the system gets to see.

Here's the ugly speculation: corporations do the government's bidding because it protects their empire. Obeying unofficial censorship orders earns them favor. Disobedience risks regulatory punishment, loss of federal contracts, or being branded as a platform for "harmful content."[44]

The incentives are clear in the real world: comply, censor, and get paid—or resist and become a target.

So, when you talk to AI, post a comment, or search for the 'truth' online, you're not just dealing with a tech company. You're staring into a partnership—a cross-sector alliance that decides which thoughts are safe and which ones are dangerous.

And you were never invited to that meeting.

One Last Warning for Your Shield

Before we close, there's one final irony worth flagging.

The same institutions that distort your reality now claim to teach you how to defend against misinformation. It's a bait-and-switch.

They create the noise, and then offer to train you in how to filter it.

Take "media literacy." Sounds useful. But most programs don't teach you to think critically. They teach you **which sources to obey**. The goal isn't independent analysis—it's brand loyalty to state-approved narratives.

---

43 Mark Sweney, "Mark Zuckerberg Says White House 'Pressured' Facebook to Censor Covid-19 Content," The Guardian, August 27, 2024, https://www.theguardian.com/technology/article/2024/aug/27/mark-zuckerberg-says-white-house-pressured-facebook-to-censor-covid-19-content.

44 Ibid

Then there's "pre-bunking." Instead of letting you weigh ideas for yourself, it poisons the well in advance, framing certain viewpoints as dangerous or ridiculous before you even hear them. That's not education. That's psychological priming.

The result? You're handed a toolkit to resist manipulation, **but it's been designed by the manipulators themselves.**

These programs aren't building independent thinkers.
They're building people who comply by reflex.

So, here's the final principle to carry with you:

If a system teaches you HOW to resist propaganda, that's great! If it teaches you WHO to listen to ... scrutinize that system (including the system proposed in this very book).

Final Thoughts: The Shield Is Yours Now

You've made it. From historical case studies to modern-day censorship systems, you've now seen how the propaganda machine was built—and how it's evolving. The lies are smarter. The delivery systems are faster. But the tactics? Still the same.

At the beginning of this book, we made a simple claim: **Propaganda works best when you don't know it's happening.** Now you do.

The shield you've built isn't made of steel or stone—it's made of awareness. That alone puts you ahead of most people. You've learned how to spot manipulation, question the framing, and think upstream. But most importantly, you've learned that no one is coming to rescue your mind from this fog. You have to do it yourself.

So, what now?

- **Limit exposure** to attention traps and algorithmic opinion shapers.
- **Talk with others**—help them see what you now see.
- **Keep the shield up**. Even when it's subtle. Especially when it's subtle.

The fog is thick out there. But you have a compass now. Use it.

Key Takeaways: Chapter 37

1. **Governments Outsource Censorship**
   The U.S. government often avoids direct suppression by partnering with tech companies, nonprofits, and contractors to quietly and without oversight dampen or erase speech.

2. **Exposure = Persuasion**
   What's visible shapes your worldview. What's hidden might as well not exist. AI, search engines, and social platforms are now the gatekeepers of attention.

3. **AI Isn't Neutral**
   Classifiers, metaprompts, provenance tools, and hidden moderation systems quietly control what answers you're allowed to receive—even if you don't see it happening.

4. **Corporations Are Willing Middlemen**
   Big Tech censors because it benefits them: government favor, protection, and money. It's not "resilience to misinformation." It's empire maintenance.

5. **Media Literacy & Pre-Bunking Are Tools of Control**
   "Approved outlet" checklists and psychological pre-biasing tactics don't educate—they indoctrinate. Your thoughts are pre-sorted before you even form them.

YOU'RE INVITED!

It's time to shield our families and communities from the destructive pull of propaganda...together.

You don't have to fight this battle alone. Through the new Propaganda Shield community forums, you can discuss the teaching tools and strategies that will sharpen your understanding and strengthen your defenses.

I've created forums where we can engage with ideas, challenge each other, and sharpen our thinking together. You'll also find additional teaching resources designed to make the lessons in this book come alive in practical, everyday ways.

Last but not least: most of the world's problems are fueled by propaganda—and too many people don't even know it. If this message is going to change the world, it can't stop with you. I need your help to get the word out. We NEED our friends, family, and neighbors more con-proof. Share the book, discuss it with your friends, and invite others into the fight. Every person who wakes up to how propaganda works makes all of us stronger.

As I often remind parents and leaders, knowledge without action is just information. The real power comes when we put what we've learned into practice—and when we spread it.

Step into the discussion at

propagandashield.com/community

If you want to dive deeper into the materials you just read about (where I teach video lectures and video examples of concepts we've discussed in this book). Go here for a discount:

https://propagandashield.com/reader-offer

Write me anytime and tell me how you're using these tools and spreading the word at: **wilson@propagandashield.com.**

Thanks again for being a part of the solution. Godspeed.

With determination,

Wilson Stooksberry

ABOUT THE AUTHOR

Wilson is a former special operations veteran with 20 years of experience and over a decade of teaching under his belt. For more than two decades, he's traveled the globe studying propaganda—drawing on formal military training, hundreds of books, thousands of hours of interviews, and real-world analysis. His insights reached broad audiences, which helped him realize his calling to create resources on propaganda awareness.

His work in curriculum development, teaching, and public speaking has taken him across the world; first instructing military and medical professionals in high-stakes environments, and now equipping communities to recognize and resist propaganda wherever it appears.

Wilson's mission is to help people see through manipulation and reclaim clarity. His work speaks to parents who want to safeguard their children, to teachers committed to critical thinking, to mentors guiding the next generation, and to every citizen determined not to be gaslit by a culture that rewards compliance over truth.

For speaking invitations, podcast appearances, or media inquiries, email ***media@propagandashield.com***